typography

by Aaron Burns

Library of Congress Catalog Card No. 61-14822

Printed in the United States of America

© 1961, Reinhold Publishing Corporation

 REINHOLD PUBLISHING CORPORATION, New York

1ne
2wo
3hree
4our
5ive
6ix
7even
8ight
9ine
10n
11even

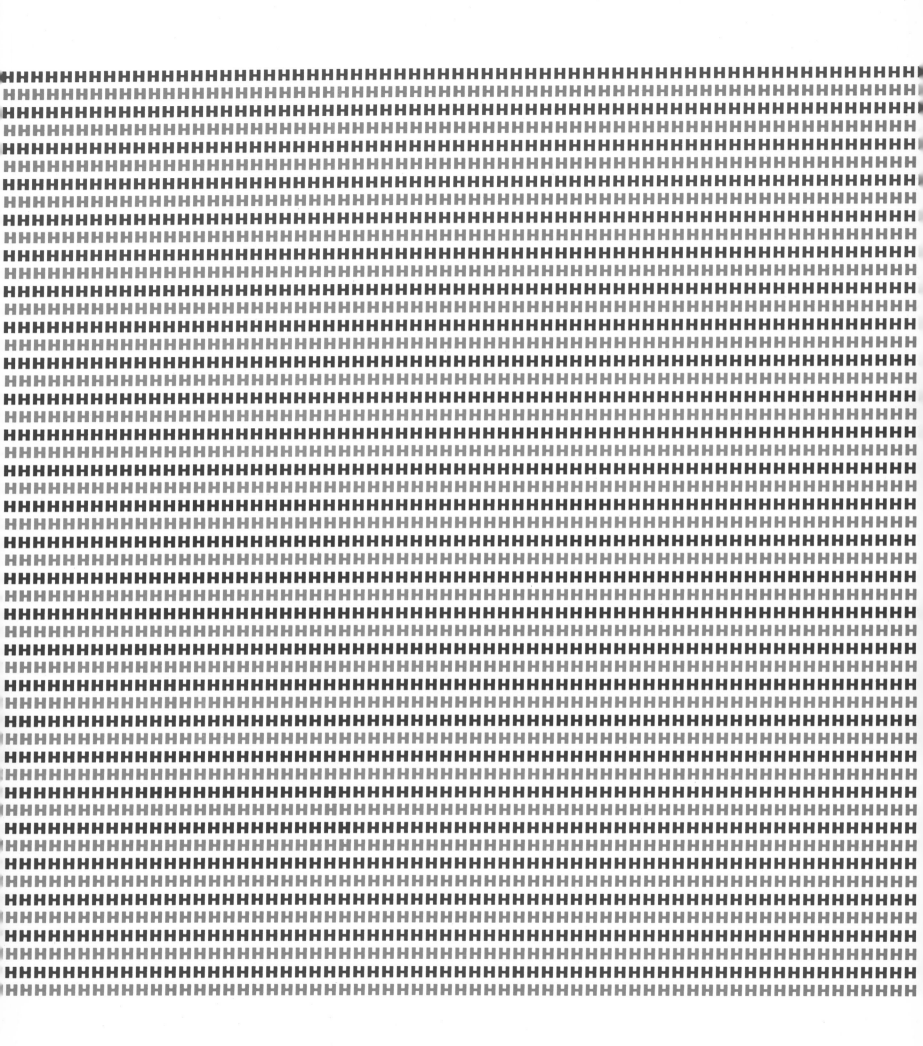

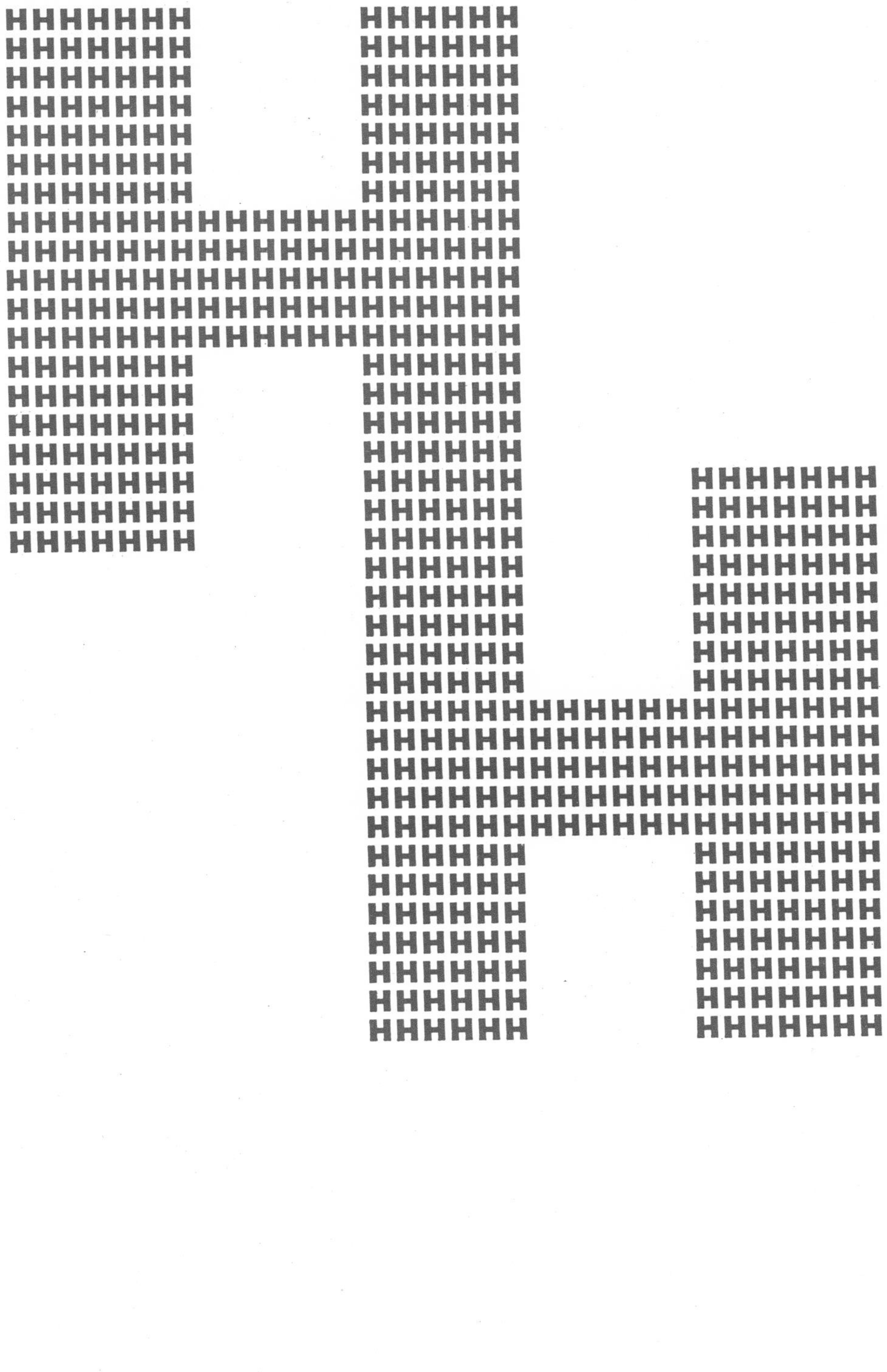

Nitranitol with Rauwolfia *provides* tandem action for *safe*, gradual, prolonged relief: Nitranitol for prompt *relief* of distressing symptoms *and* slower-acting Rauwolfia (alseroxylon fraction) for *prolonged* hypotensive and quieting *action*—no lag *in* symptom relief. The combination means normal life sooner for your essential *hypertension* patients...no jolting of the vasomotor reflexes...side effects are uncommon. Other Nitranitol dosage forms include Nitranitol, Nitranitol with Phenobarbital, Nitranitol with Phenobarbital and Rutin, Nitranitol with Phenobarbital and Theophylline, and Nitranitol P.V.

DOSE: 2 TABS. Q.I.D. FOR B.P. OVER 200 SYSTOLIC; OTHERS 1 OR 2 TABS. Q. 4-6H.

T.M. NITRANITOL®, 'NITRANITOL P.V.' AND 'NITRANITOL R.S.'

The Wm. S. Merrell Company • St. Thomas, Ont., CINCINNATI, New York • Pioneer in Medicine for Over 125 Years

CINEMA
REX

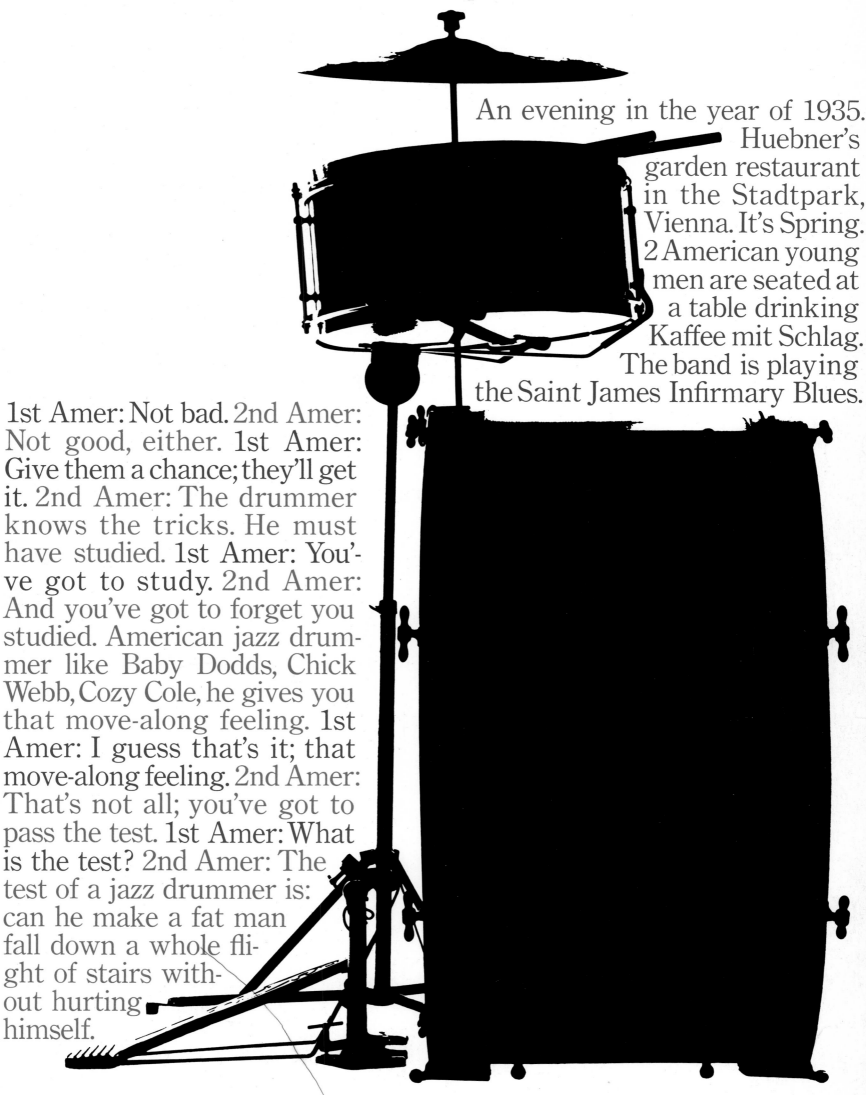

Über die Philosophie der Kunst.

An evening in the year of 1935. Huebner's garden restaurant in the Stadtpark, Vienna. It's Spring. 2 American young men are seated at a table drinking Kaffee mit Schlag. The band is playing the Saint James Infirmary Blues.

1st Amer: Not bad. 2nd Amer: Not good, either. 1st Amer: Give them a chance; they'll get it. 2nd Amer: The drummer knows the tricks. He must have studied. 1st Amer: You've got to study. 2nd Amer: And you've got to forget you studied. American jazz drummer like Baby Dodds, Chick Webb, Cozy Cole, he gives you that move-along feeling. 1st Amer: I guess that's it; that move-along feeling. 2nd Amer: That's not all; you've got to pass the test. 1st Amer: What is the test? 2nd Amer: The test of a jazz drummer is: can he make a fat man fall down a whole flight of stairs without hurting himself.

enkele gegevens

```
                                              s
                                              sss
                           personeel 1960     sssss        staf
                                              s
                                              a
                                              aaa
                                              aaaaa          administratie
                           aaaaa aaaaa aaaaa
                           ppppp ppppp ppppp   practisch personeel
                           ppppp ppppp ppppp
                           ppppp ppppp ppppp
                           ppppp ppppp ppppp
                                 ppp
                                 wwwww          werksters
                                 wwwww
                           vvvvv vvvvv vvvvv    inventarisatie
                                 vvv
                                 v
```

bezoek   m = 10000 bezoekers

```
1959  mmmmm mmmmm mmmmm mmmmm mmmmm
  58  mmmmm mmmmm mmmmm mmmmm mmmmm m
  57  mmmmm mmmmm mmmmm mmmmm m
  56  mmmmm mmmmm mmmmm mmmmm mmmmm mmmmm mmmmm mm
  55  mmmmm mmmmm mmmmm mmm
  54  mmmmm mmmmm mmmmm mm
  53  mmmmm mmmmm mmmmm mmmmm mm
  52  mmmmm mmmmm mmmmm m
  51  mmmmm mmmmm m
  50  mmmmm mmmmm
  49  mmmmm mmmmm
  48  mmmmm mmmmm m
  47  mmmmm mmmmm mmm
  46  mmmmm mmmmm
```

tussen 1945 en 1960 werd
de dienst der gemeentemusea
uitgebreid met de volgende
afdelingen:
prentencabinet
industriele vormgeving
hedendaagse photografie
bibliotheek
leeszaal
reproductieafdeling
boekhouding
restauratie atelier
photografisch atelier
inventarisatie
   van het gehele gemeentelijk
   kunstbezit, in- en buiten
   de musea

```
                           s     staf
                           ss
        personeel 1945     aaa    administratie
                           ppppp
                           ppppp  practisch personeel
                           ppppp
                           ppppp
                           w      werklieden/werksters
                           www
                           w
```

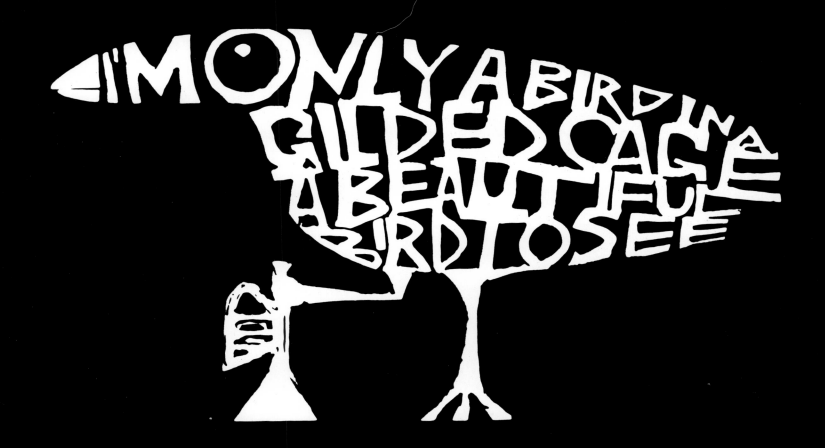

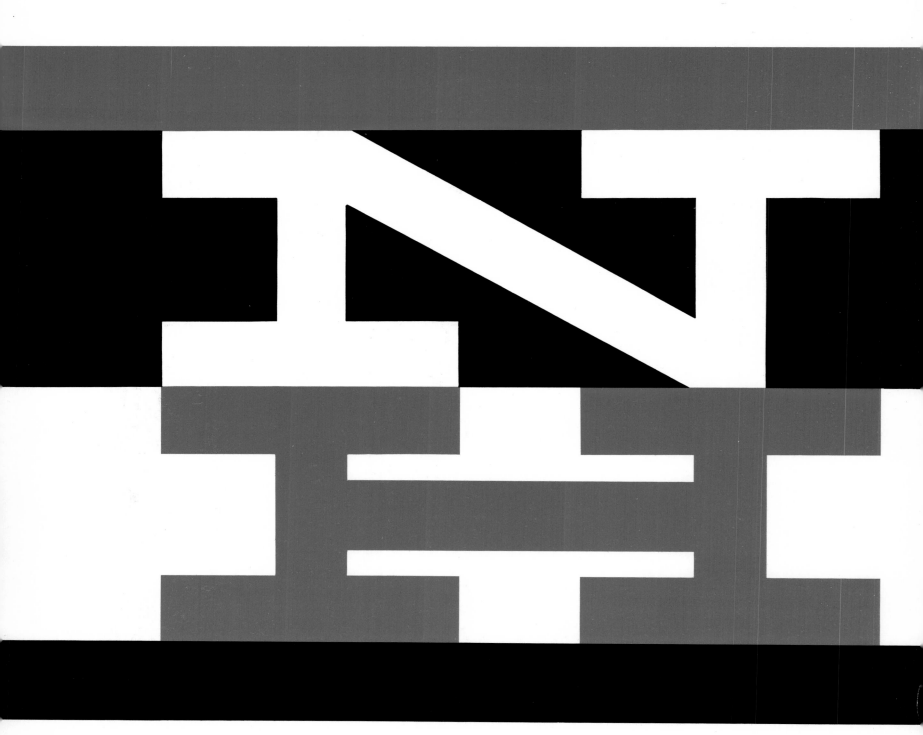

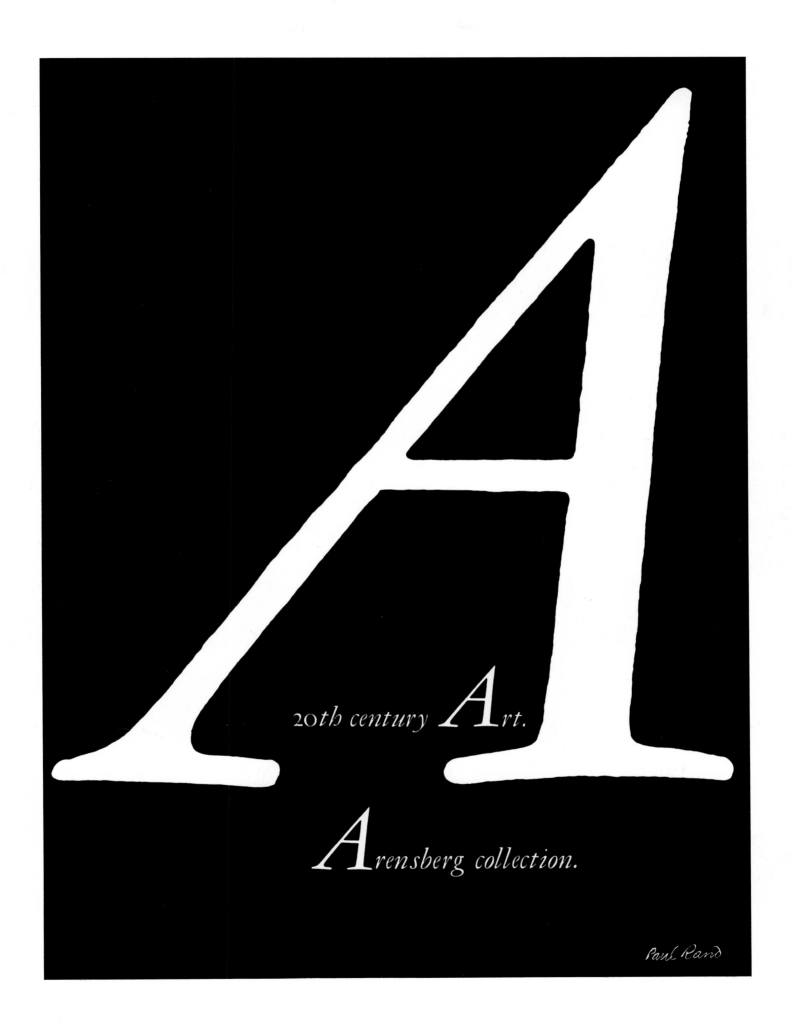

20th century *A*rt.

*A*rensberg collection.

Paul Rand

HEARING

preface This book has been planned for the student, professional and lay person, for anyone who wishes to learn more of the new function of modern typography—and the factors that contribute to its development.

Knowledge and courage are required to achieve the best results in typography. It is as true in this field as in any other that "one receives what one deserves and one deserves whatever one accepts." Fine typography is the result of nothing more than an attitude. Its appeal comes from the understanding used in its planning; the designer must care.

In contemporary advertising the "perfect" integration of design elements often demands unorthodox typography. It may require using "wrong" fonts, cutting hyphens in half, using smaller than normal punctuation marks; in fact, doing anything that is needed to improve appearance and impact.

Stating specific principles or guides on the subject of typography is difficult because one principle does not necessarily apply from one job to the next, for no two jobs are ever really alike—even though the same point sizes and typefaces are used.

Although the reader will find no rules or laws within these pages (it is my belief that the only laws that guide good typography are those of natural environment), there is sound instruction in the careful analysis of the typographic problems shown, as well as guidance and inspirational stimulus in the examples of fine typography.

I have directed and observed the execution of thousands of typographic jobs. I have seen countless behind-the-scenes developments that have transformed undistinguished pieces of typography into beautifully integrated units of color. I have seen fine craftsmanship restore order out of chaos, often due to a compositor's skill or an art director's or designer's demand for typographic quality and improvement.

Therefore in this volume I have presented many examples of such typographic refinement. And here, perhaps, is the primary purpose of this book: to teach the reader through exposure to vivid black-and-white examples of pure typography.

Almost all of the "exposure" pages are shown as they looked in their original proof form, just as they looked to the client when he first received them from the typographer. I have purposely refrained from showing the final appearance of the examples used because of the possibility that such elaboration might have a trend-setting or style-creating influence. That is not the purpose of this book. Therefore nothing has been done to improve the appearance of these specimens, no color, photography, or unusual layout treatment has been added. Wherever possible, each proof has been centered symmetrically on the page to give as much breathing space to the typography as possible. It is the author's hope that this design format will encourage the reader to concentrate on the typography before him rather than on the arrangement of the pages. The specimens themselves are responsible for whatever success the layout may have.

It is worthwhile to emphasize here that in modern typography almost all typefaces, old or new, are utilized. Modern typography, with its emphasis on simplicity and brevity, does not consider any good typeface to be dated. On the contrary, as the examples clearly demonstrate, a simple letter a hundred or more years old may combine well with a most recent face, as does serif and sans serif, script and gothic. In short, there should be no rule except to make typography pleasing to the eye.

Aaron Burns

introduction Typography as a communication medium takes many directions and acquires many forms. It is important to differentiate between new and successful solutions and mere trends or style-setting fashions. In typography, Function is of major importance, Form is secondary, and Fashion almost meaningless.

Some of these areas of application are identified in order to help the reader become aware of the many purposes for which typography is used, and so recognize unmistakably the differences in Function, Form and Fashion. The following comments discuss the examples shown on pages 5 to 16. Look at the examples themselves to see how the layout (FORM), and the choice of typefaces (FASHION), were used to implement the most important element—the design idea (FUNCTION) that solved the problem.

Page 5 is an example of the experimental use of typography. The negative forms and the ingenious use of numerals as parts of words, compel the reader to study the message carefully to be sure that there is no more to the page than meets the eye. Thus experimental typography very often can be utilized to add further depths of interest and meaning to a page.

Page 6 is an example of typographic "texture." We often speak of type color as having texture. The weights and curves of certain letters create different textures. The beauty of letters when multiplied and grouped as shown on this page can create very interesting patterns and textures. Out of such textures can be created typographic "forms." The example shown on page 7 is one of the many possibilities that can be developed.

Pages 8, 9 and 10 are examples of integrated typography. On page 8 both headline and text have been integrated into one form. Size and color of type create the separation between headline and text. The examples on pages 9 and 10 show the integration of individual strokes, letters and words to create additional forms of unusual interest and excitement.

Page 11 is a solution to the problem of dialogue interpretation. Color has been utilized to separate conversation. Color in typography, therefore, can assume additional functions other than the more familiar purpose of beauty and adornment.

On page 12 typography has been used to transmit statistical information. The use of type characters to represent percentages and degrees of information is a new and successful solution to this difficult problem.

Page 13 is an example of figurative letterform. Figurative typography is a form of illustration or painting in which letters and words are arranged into shapes of objects. Used intelligently, figurative typography can create interesting animation and spark highly imaginative designs.

Page 14 is an example of the use of typography for identification purposes. The use of typographic letters to denote corporate identity through trademarks and logotypes has become a successful solution to many ''image-building'' problems.

Page 15 shows the relationship and association of letter-forms to content. Very often key words in the text start with similar letters that have similar connotations. The association of these words and objects in letter-forms often permits dynamic solutions.

Some words inspire their own solution, as in the example shown on page 16. Such solutions often combine several of the functions of typography mentioned above to create unusual and imaginative results.

typographic design Because today's ever-increasing world population must be kept informed of the enormous strides being made in science, technology and industry, we are now faced with the task of disseminating more information to more people than ever before. And this must be done largely through secondary mediums of communication: radio, television and printed matter. This book deals with one of the secondary mediums of communication—typography.

Today, typography surrounds us—in signs, in architecture, in books and magazines, and on television. In short, we find typography wherever and whenever ideas and information are communicated graphically.

Most of us think of typography as existing in two distinct and unrelated areas—as a medium for transmitting knowledge (books and magazines) and as a medium for selling products or communicating ideas and information (advertising and publicity). Most published material on the principles of typography has been concerned with book typography, which is based on natural laws. Books are meant to be read; we all know that anything that detracts from this fundamental purpose is poor book typography.

However, advertising typography, typography for packages, architecture, industrial design, television, billboards and so forth is communication of a very different kind. Paradoxical as it may seem, we have learned that some typographic messages need not always be completely read or even clearly understood. On a poster or billboard the message is to be scanned quickly rather than read and digested slowly. It is considered successful if the reader remembers only the logotype or the name of the product or client.

"Image impact" and "dynamism" have become new functions for typography. "Type is to be read" seems to be a bent axiom. Today's advertising asks far more of typographic design than the job of communicating information.

Much modern typography startles, identifies, charms, and even illustrates. Designers prime little typographic explosions to go off with a flash and a visual noise at the turning of a page. The life expectancy of these messages can be measured in seconds, or fractions of seconds. The hope is that the small detonations will blast the reader's mind open long enough to imprint an image or an idea, as opposed to a message. Whether or not the explosion is actually read seems to be secondary to its being seen and heard. Even though we may not wish to accept this new function of modern typography, we must admit that it exists.

New messages born out of new problems have created new forms. New designers born in the aftermath of the German Bauhaus and the Dutch DeStijl movements created new "exposures," a typography of the moment—bold, clear and with stature. This new typography can be characterized best by three words: SIMPLICITY . . . SPACE . . . STRENGTH.

Since the physical structure of typography is made up of words, typographic form depends upon the kind of words used. It is important that the word have something to communicate and do so directly and simply. Quantity of content affects form—quality of content determines result.

What then is typographic design? One definition is "typography is to printing as dramatics and elocution are to the spoken word."

How then can we communicate an idea typographically?

How can we inform people, convince them, persuade them to accept or refuse, buy or sell, do something or do nothing, with just word messages and word pictures?

In order to explore this problem further we should examine the developmental pattern of a typical typographic problem. Let us begin first with the typewritten manuscript copy. Here in this first stage, we have only the monotone of typewritten letters. We have no advantage of typefaces with their style and color. However, first, even before the manuscript copy, there must be the IDEA. Here then is where we really begin. What is an idea?

An idea is a design for action. It is a plan, a thought, a concept. Layout is only an arrangement for the plan, the design, the idea or concept. And inherent in every problem are the seeds of its solution.

A typographic idea is almost always an inspirational or creative effort. Layout is usually an interpretive one.

When we see something in print that is all type and is visually exciting, we very often fail to credit the writer or author of the idea for the inspiration he has provided for the designer. We fail to recognize that the solution to the problem has almost always been dictated by the words themselves.

For example, the following illustration, "private secretary," is an excellent example of typographic design. The problem assigned to the designer was to create a visual title for a television program. The solution describes perfectly the kind of "private secretary" appearing on that program. The choice of a typewriter face was automatic once the designer decided to solve the problem typographically. The layout or placement of the type, no matter how badly arranged, could not seriously harm the success of the idea or solution—the idea was too strong. This was a most vivid description of a very inefficient private secretary.

Some words spark typographic imagination and produce inspired results. Others provide little or no stimulus to the designer and it is almost always in these instances that typographic acrobatics come into being to lend visual excitement to tired words. However, no amount of typographic styling can ever change the meaning of words; it can only make them look different. It is the form that changes, not the content. Quite obviously the content is the most important.

On the following pages are some excellent examples of simple but dynamic copy. With the aid of good typographic design and layout, these messages give outstanding visual performances.

At the back of the book, comments pertinent to each page shown in the "exposure" section will be made. Many of them bear upon styling points that are considered significant; in several cases examples of imperfect typography are deliberately shown.

Careful, constant, painstaking care and attention to every detail is necessary to achieve "perfect" typography. Although the effort is great—the reward is greater still for those who **care!**

---

pxixt

private

   secreatary

. . . .

CBS televitsiokn

This is an example of "pure" typographic design. Had the designer used any other typeface than the one most commonly found on a typewriter, it would have reduced the clarity of the message.

WE
BEGIN
WITH
APPLES—
BECAUSE
THEY
HAVE
SUCH
LOVELY
NAMES:

UNIQUE

Often the intelligent use of typography can make one word worth a thousand pictures in communicating the special qualities of your product or service. This is one way a high graphic IQ can make your image stand out from the kaleidoscope of competitive claims. Clients of SH&L judge the excellence of its typographic design by its proven ability to pass the rigorous test of the market place. Call Herb Lubalin at PL 1-1250 and let's talk type among other things.

allergic
SWELLING

Dimetane® works
(PARABROMDYLAMINE MALEATE)

For your next patient with swelling, itching or respiratory congestion associated with urticaria, Rx DIMETANE Extentabs® (12 mg.), Tablets (4 mg.), Elixir (2 mg./5 cc.) DIMETANE-TEN Injectable (10 mg./cc.) or DIMETANE-100 Injectable (100 mg./cc.).

One of the last things a driver thinks about while thre[...]
through today's frenetic traffic is how long the manufactu[...]
his choice has been in business. This little nugget of inform[...]
on first thought, would seem to have little to do with how[...]
the car goes. On reflection, however, and in connection wit[...]
Rover 3-Litre to be examined here, it has a great deal to do[...]
the performance and appearance of an auto firm's end proc[...]
Only two other U.S. car builders—Ford and Olds—can matc[...]
Rover Company's 56 continuous years of designing and [...]
cating automobiles. In many ways the newest Rover re[...]
traditional thinking—solid rear axle, chair-high seating, F[...]
engine—while in others—laminated torsion bar front suspe[...]
monocoque chassis, disc brakes—it is abreast of, if not ahea[...]
contemporary engineering. A modern aspect of the 3-Litre[...]
body shape. Externally it owes much to the Italian scho[...]
design, suitably worked around in front to retain—though fa[...]
—some flavor of the traditional Rover grille. This marriage [...]
Latin line and British conservatism has been tried on one o[...]
other English luxury cars in the past. The results, unfortun[...]
have not produced a lasting union. The 3-Litre, however, [...]
to be a happy combination of both schools of thought, one[...]
we think will wear well. Attaining a modern appearance[...]
would not offend old-line Rover owners must have been o[...]
the more difficult jobs faced by the engineering staff when[...]
laid out the new car. Down through the years Rover cars [...]
been adopted by some of Britain's better families. A new n[...]
in vulgar taste would be tantamount to having a young son[...]
down from Oxford for slovenly dress. This deference to[...]
tastes of past Rover buyers gives a clue to the type of car[...]
the company has been building for the past half century. R[...]
have been solid, dependable, unostentatious automobiles[...]
quietly inform driver and passengers alike that they are ridi[...]
a luxury car. This same impression is given onlookers a[...]
Rover goes silently by.

The new 3-Litre in no way differs from this established appr[...]
Entrance through the 36-inch wide front door opening ca[...]
accomplished without loss of dignity or breath. The first [...]

We take pleasure in reprinting the accompanying appreciation of the Rover 3-Litre Sedan by the editors of Sports Cars Illustrated. We believe that it will help define, for the interested motorist, the unique qualities that have endeared the Rover to generations of owners.

ROVER

THE ROVER MOTOR COMPANY OF
NORTH AMERICA LIMITED
36-12 37th Street, Long Island City 1,
New York / 373 Shaw Road, South
San Francisco, Calif. / Mobile
Drive, Toronto, Ontario,
Canada / 156 W. Second
Ave., Vancouver, B.C.,
Canada

that strikes a neophyte Rover driver when he gets behind[...]
wheel is that this is a big car. Its wheelbase is only 7.5 in[...]
less than the latest Plymouth, yet overall length is 22.5 in[...]
less than the same be-finned U.S. sedan. The next thing that[...]
notices is the quality of workmanship displayed in the inte[...]
trim. For one attuned to the vagaries of production-line t[...]
niques employed on small economy sedans, the Rover inte[...]
impresses by its lack of sharp points, ragged edges, and sl[...]
measure head linings. Adding to this feeling of richness are[...]
real leather upholstery and walnut-faced door fillets and g[...]
compartment lids.

The pleasantly thick-rimmed steering wheel is set at just a[...]
the right angle and does not project into the driver's lin[...]

ht, while the instrument binnacle is positioned high enough allow readings to be taken without consciously having to e one's eyes from the road. This instrument pod, cowled to ninate reflections, contains dials for speed, water temperature, l and oil levels, switches for panel lights (with brightness itrol) main lights, oil level and key start ignition lock. Warn-; lights, placed between the two big dials, are used to indicate k of oil pressure and sparks. With the exception of the cold rt device—manual choke with an amber light that warns en it's in use, and the oil level gadget that utilizes the fuel ige pointer when the right switch is flicked to give a rough imate of the amount of oil in the sump—all of these instru-nts can be found on many other cars. What you don't find, wever, is the quality of workmanship that makes everything the Rover work with such a degree of smoothness that you d yourself clicking things on and off just to look and listen.

e seating position (our test car had the bench seat—bucket ts can be had as optional extras) is very comfortable with emphasis on giving a driver of more than average size nty of room. Distaff drivers (that most American women ve is a fact that has to be faced) might find the driving seat t a little too commodious. The fold-down arm rest cuts the -inch-wide front seat roughly in half, thus limiting the dis-ice that the smaller driver will slide on the smooth leather, t it still leaves a generous space for the small-derriered to tle around in. Gears are shifted in the four-speed box by a oked lever that projects, after suitable bends, from under the -wide parcel shelf. It is shaped so as not to discommode a itral passenger. After getting the gear shift lever very neatly of the way, it seems a shame that the rather large transmis-n tunnel does encroach on the foot room of the middle pas-ger. In use the gearbox fits the temperament of the Rover to .. Strong, blocker-type synchromesh prevents ultra-fast shifts, ile making normal shifts simple and silent. On our test car detent spring that prevents accidental engagement of reverse en one is going for first gear was a little weak. This proved ninor embarrassment on one occasion. Rover drivers should never appear flustered to people in lesser vehicles.

With a twist of the ignition key the 182-cubic-inch six is ready to go. When cold there is just the slight-est amount of valve noise. After the engine is warm you have to use the ignition warning light to find out whether or not you've stalled. (An aside on the amount of time it takes for the 3-Litre to warm up: Apparently Rover owners are not expected to

e in cold cars. Within blocks the very nprehensive heating system is pouring warm air.) Under way the Rover im-sses by its silence. Up to 45 or 50 mph you hear the electric clock ticking. At speeds over t, wind noise—right around the center door post—muffles sound of the clock, but doesn't intrude on conversation ried on at a living room level of pitch and volume. On open road the Rover reveals its reason for being. At speed steering that seemed heavy in slow crawling traffic is ht and precise, while the big, roomy seats allow plenty of geting space. It is easy to visualize a captain of industry hur-ng from one end of England to the other on important busi-

ness in the comfort of his Rover. Ride is just a little firmer than on domestic sedans, which does away with that floating sensa-tion you sometimes get in softly sprung cars at turnpike speeds. Bumps, with the softer suspension of the 3-Litre, are over and done with without the series of diminishing oscillations familiar to users of American-built luxury cars. Cornering—or just plain handling—is good for any situation that a Rover user might find himself in. Tires do howl on tight corners if recommended pressures are adhered to, and the car understeers to a greater and greater degree as speeds into turns are increased.

The Rover brakes are more than a little responsible for the car's ability to put up high averages. When first tried we thought they were a little puny to cope with the 3-Litre's 4,000-odd pounds of bulk. This, however, was a case of familiarity breeding satisfac-tion. It was also an interesting case of how preconditioned senses can mislead. In 90 percent of the automobiles being built today one sign of husky brakes doing their job is the sight of the nose of the car dipping violently. This is not what happens with the Rover, however. When the stop pedal is pushed the car simply stops—without dipping, swaying or swerving—it just stops. Few of the effects of deceleration are transmitted to the occupants. One simple way to achieve this non-dipping quality is by tipping the front wishbones up slightly, which is what the Rover people have done. All of the above commentary was based on the brakes of our test car, which were drum-type all around. Newer 3-Litre cars are equipped with Girling discs on the front which should make braking capabilities that much better.

The empathy between buyers and builder is nowhere better displayed than in the very comprehensive owner's manual that accompanies every Rover car. Its tone is that of two old friends having a chat over a good dinner. . . . If the unthinkable should happen and a Rover owner came to an unscheduled halt, ten well-made hand tools reside in a form-fitting sponge rubberlined tray that slides out from under the parcel shelf. If it's only a flat tire, however, a jack, lug wrench, tire pump and spare tire valve in a little lidded depression can be found in the trunk—all se-curely fastened to prevent rattles, of course. For a flat battery a crank is also clipped on the side of the trunk. All of these things, along with the very well-written owner's manual, should make a Rover driver fairly self-sufficient. A delivered price of about $5,000* makes the 3-Litre Rover an expensive car to buy. However, purchase of a Rover is the nearest an individual can come to buying a friend. —SCI May, 1960

*Prices of the Rover 3-Litre Sedan vary with ports of entry and equipment. It is available with Borg-Warner automatic transmis-sion as well as four-speed gearbox with overdrive.

He blow; he don't worry...
There's this cat he knows
Wingy from 'way back.
But he's a sadistic &
a square, not that it
matter to Wingy
Malone, he
got only one
arm. He
blow;
he don't
worry.
Each year
this guy
send Wingy
his Christ–
mas present
in a fancy box:
one cuff link!

PARA-
BOLIC
BORE:/
OLD JAZZ
NEED NOT
BE BEST BUT
STILL IT'S TRUE
THAT SAXOPHONES
WERE FEW AND FAR
BETWEEN IN GOOD
KING PORTER'S MERRY
TIMES. THOSE WHO DO
NOT LOVE THE SOUND
THAT ISSUES FROM THE
BLEND OF BRASS-
BENT HORN WITH
WOODEN REED
ARE THREATEN-
ED IN THESE
PARTS, BUT
THEY'RE
AROU-
ND!

"Check you at Linga Longa."

We made it over the Jefferson Davis Highway in a Model-T some 200 miles south of Richmond, Virginia in the State of North Carolina, a couple of 18-year-old kids. The back of the open touring car was loaded with ponchos, pup tents, army blankets and cans of Van Camp's pork and beans. I had a pen knife that was an arsenal in the pocket: two cutting blades, a can-opener, a bottle-opener and a corkscrew. I had never before in my life been south of Philadelphia nor heard of Brunswick stew. The girls walking along Fayetville Street were unbelievable. Corn silk, they made me think of. I could not take my eyes off them. Were these the southern belles I had read about? That night, we saw Norma Talmadge, Conway Tearle and Wallace Berry in "Ashes of Vengeance" at the Superba Theatre, college kids in the audience, hissing the villain. The next day was Saturday and in the afternoon my Carolina cousin Fed (short for Confederate), two of his school friends and the two of us piled into the Ford and went checkin'. Checkin' was riding up and down the wide street bordering the campus as the girls either sat on the curb of the lawn or promenaded within limits. (Echoes of courtship in Granada?) On Saturday afternoon, everybody went checkin', mainly to arrange for more checkin' later on. "Check you at Linga Longa," one of the boys called out to a honey blonde. Linga Longa, seemed to be the place. That's what they kept saying: Linga Longa. Saturday night, we put on our white pants and blue blazers and drove through cotton fields and scrub pine to Linga Longa. But the sign said Linger Longer. Southern talk had thrown me. Linger Longer was a kind of lake resort featuring an outdoor dance pavilion in a pine grove. The floor was jammed with dancers and boys cutting in, the first I ever saw of that practice. Band was a piano, trumpet, trombone, clarinet, banjo, drums—Negro musicians. "Ja Da," familiar to jazz since World War One, was the old-shoe favorite: Ja da, Ja da, jada jada jing, jing, jing . . . a strain, really, like so many great jazz vehicles. Then "Sister Kate" did her shimmy, "Wang Wang Blues" cut out, followed by "Indiana" and "Everybody Loves My Baby but My Baby Loves Nobody but Me." Six of us on the way home in the Model-T, and checkin' achieved its objective of neckin'. At eighteen, we had already won the grand prize: full possession of the hour. Did I dream all this?

ugh!'ly?

Ugliness, like beauty, is in the eye of the beholder. It is a value imposed upon a thing which, properly used, might well be called beautiful. At **S H & L** we try to avoid misleading labels. Our business is to design for advertising. Typography is one of our essential tools. If what we do with it is effective, we don't care if it is called pretty, ugly, or pretty ugly. If you think as we do, we ought to get together. Call Herb Lubalin at Plaza 1-1250, where we take the ugh**!** out of ugly.

ugh!'ly?

CONNEE BOSWELL

AND THE ORIGINAL MEMPHIS FIVE IN HI-FI

I.M
11/15
AT
G.H*

Guild House brings a new fashion message to Coral Gables

The
emotional and
social pressures which in
tensify overeating proble
may vary considerably in y
obese patients. With some
attempt of dieting itself can
additional stress. Therapeut
sound individualization of
obesity regimens is theref
desirable, but — as has b
established — more easi
achieved with the three
different forms of
Ambar.[1]

s
ur
he
use
ally
nti-
re
n

for
the
successful
treatment
of
obesity
"Dosage
must
be
manipulated
to
suit
the
individual
patient."[1]
simply
achieved
with
the
different
forms
of
Ambar™

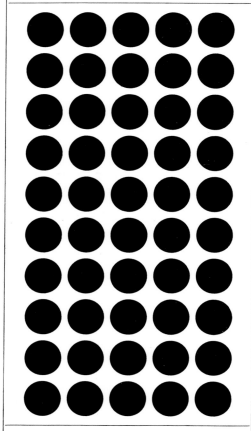

from King County Hospital, Seattle, Wash.

"Summary of weight control program in 50 obese patients in whom Ambar dosage was individualized. Side reaction rate for the total 80 patients studied was only 5%—as reported and illustrated in NORTHWEST MEDICINE[1]

44 averaged 18.4 lbs.'weight loss

Stopped medication— side reactions

Gained or failed to lose

1. Barnes, R. H.: Northwest Med. 57:1011, 1958.

The Difference Between a Dress and a L'Aiglon Is the Way You Look!

A *all this...*
AMSTERDAM

BARCELONA

BIRMINGHAM

BLACKPOOL

BRISTOL

𝕭𝕽𝖀𝕾𝕾𝕰𝕷𝕾

CARDIFF

COPENHAGEN

DUSSELDORF

EDINBURGH

𝕱𝕽𝕬𝕹𝕶𝕱𝕺𝕽𝕿

GLASGOW

LISBON

LIVERPOOL

LONDON

LOURDES

MANCHESTER

NEWCASTLE-ON-TYNE

PARIS

ROME

Z URICH

...and Ireland, too!

Jubilee . . . sparkling as champagne. The look of precious stones, the look of crystal, crystal aurora, ruby aurora, fresh water pearl
or Vitrail with gold-colored settings; in ice blue or starlight with silver-colored settings.
Necklace, bracelet, pin, earrings: each, $2 *plus tax. At fine stores everywhere.*

All designs copyright 1958 D. **L**isner *& Co.,* 393 *Fifth Avenue, New York*

This
flair
for flattery.
This finesse
with figures.
The neat jacket comes off
to reveal a fashion
gay enough for a party!
In houndstooth checked
Dacron to wash, drip-dry
and not iron!
Black and white (shown);
navy and white.
Sizes 5 to 15.
$22.95.
this
is

SELECTED WORKS 2

THE

MUSEUM
OF PRIMITIVE
ART

**THAT'S
WHAT
HE SAID,
WHEN
ASKED**

**IN A GREENWICH VILLAGE NIGHT CLUB, FATS W
FINISHED PLAYING AND SINGING HIS WAY THROU
TWENTY-MINUTE SET WHICH INCLUDED HONE
SWEET GEORGIA BROWN, I'M JUST WILD ABOU
STREET BLUES, BODY AND SOUL, SOMEBODY
BLUE TURNING GRAY OVER YOU. PERSPIRING,
ING THE APPLAUSE, FATS LEFT HIS PIANO AND
TO THE BAR WHERE HE ENCOUNTERED A FASH
ED WOMAN. "OH," SHE SAID, "JUST THE MAN I W
SURE YOU CAN ANSWER MY QUESTION. TELL N
WHAT IS SWING?" FATS REACHED FOR HIS DI
HAND, MOPPED HIS FACE WITH THE OTHER, L
WOMAN SQUARELY AND REPLIED, "LADY, IF Y
YOU AINT GOT IT!" RELAXING BETWEEN SETS, A
AT A TABLE IN A FIFTY-SECOND STREET BISTRO,
FROM A BOTTLE. "BUT FAITH IS YOUR SALVAT
BROWNSKIN GIRL. AND ART TOOK A SWIG OF I
OUT IT YOU ARE LOST," SAID THE BROWNSKIN
ART TATUM SADLY SIPPED HIS BEER. "ALL GO
ARE LOST," SAID ART, "BUT ONLY A FEW CAN P**

**ART
TATUM,
1910-1957
(LOST
MAN
PLAYED
FINE
PIANO)**

ER HAD JUST
A STUNNING
CKLE ROSE,
RRY, BASIN
ES ME AND
GHING, LOV-
LKED OVER
ABLY-DRESS-
TO SEE. I'M
MR. WALLER,
K WITH ONE
KED AT THE
GOTTA ASK,
TATUM SAT
NKING BEER
," SAID THE
BEER. "WITH-
L, AS BLIND
CHILDREN
THE PIANO."

boldness and beauty
are brilliantly balanced
in new fall fabrics
by Milliken!

DIVINE TO EAT, EASY TO MAKE, AND
BEAUTIFUL TO LOOK ON: ELEGANT PAR-
FAITS. THERE ARE TWO TYPES: THE
FRENCH, WHICH IS A CREAMY, DEL-
ICATE, COOL (BUT NOT ICY) MIX-
TURE WITH A BASE OF SUGAR,
EGGS, CREAM, FRUIT AND/OR
FLAVORINGS; AND THE AMERI-
CAN, MADE WITH COMMERCIAL
ICE CREAMS OR SHERBETS OR
BOTH WITH A SURPRISE INGRE-
DIENT, SUCH AS FRUITS, COR-
DIALS, COGNAC, NUTS, SAUCES
(SEE McCALL'S FINE SAUCE
RECIPES ON PAGE 00). WITH
AMERICAN PARFAITS, YOUR
IMAGINATION CAN HAVE FREE
REIN. WITH THE FRENCH, HOW-
EVER, YOU MUST FOLLOW REC-
IPE DIRECTIONS TO THE
LETTER. PARFAIT MEANS, OF
COURSE, PERFECT, AND WE
CAN IMAGINE FEW MORE PER-
FECT DESSERTS, ESPECIALLY
IF YOU WANT TO SHOW OFF.
FOR THESE ARE TRULY SHOW-
OFF RECIPES! FROM THE
COOK'S STANDPOINT, THERE
IS A REAL ADVANTAGE IN SERV-
ING FROZEN DESSERTS. FOR
THE OBVIOUS REASON, THEY
MUST BE MADE WELL AHEAD
AND REFRIGERATED. THUS,
THE BIG DESSERT PROBLEM
IS OUT OF THE WAY WHEN IT'S
TIME TO PREPARE THE MAIN
PART OF THE MEAL. AT FAR
RIGHT, YOU SEE AN AMER-
ICAN PARFAIT, VANILLA
ICE CREAM LAYERED
WITH PISTACHIO
AND TOPPED
WITH WAL-
NUTS AND
WHIPPED
CREAM.
THE STRAW-
BERRY AND
APRICOT
PARFAITS
ARE BOTH
CLASSIC
FRENCH.
FOR THE RECIPES,
TURN TO PAGE 00, WHERE
YOU WILL FIND THE FRENCH AS WELL
AS GOOD VARIATIONS OF THE QUICK
AND POPULAR AMERICAN PARFAITS.
THEN, PLAN A PARTY.

Five fashions designed in America to out-Paris Paris! Responsible

for this magic—Gay Gibson, one of the most scintillating names in

the junior fashion world! All, in the currently relaxed silhouette . . .

in beautiful fabrics and striking autumn colors. All, in sizes 5 to 15.

For a while, the capital of everything had become the world's number one bomb target and the odds in favor of a hero's death were good. But the script was overlong and while

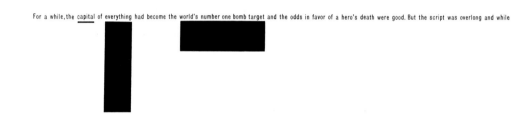

the playwrights, directors, stars and backers argued among themselves, it began to seem that the end might come, as our poet foretold, not with a bang but with a whimper

There was a time when I would detour to avoid walking anywhere on **Seven**th Avenue south of 40th to 34th. I ne**ver liked Eighth Avenue, either, and still do**n't. I have developed an affection for **Macy's no**w that The Great Department Store i**s giving way to T he Shopping Center. Wana**maker's was at its best during the years w**hich car**ried it gradually downhill to its end. I **do not understa nd those who failed to not**ice this long descent and had to be surp**rised w**hen the end came. They are childre**n who are used to being protected against** the facts of the slaughterhouse. What **great per**ception is needed to know that a de**partment store, office building or theatre is** like a tree or shrub? Yet, many do not k**now this**. I can understand the young not kn**owing because, to them, a tree seems to h**ave existed and promises to exist forev**er. But t**he middle-aged and the old? I am bo**red, too, with th e conceit that depicts hero**ic edifices such as the Brooklyn Bridge o**r the Wo**olworth Building as challenging nat**ure. They are na ture. In art, though, as in th**e forest, certain forms are destined for l**onger lif**e than others. Fortunately, man has **permitted conti nuing life to the violin, the J**ensen letter and the bicycle, despite th**e fact th**at the points of their full developme**nt have long sin ce been reached. Not so wi**th New York. New York cuts down both **its trees** and its buildings, not only long befo**re they have die d, but long before they hav**e been able to demonstrate their ability **to live. I**n the beginning of the love affair wit**h New York, ign orance of the ways of the b**eloved is bliss. At this stage, it's simply t**he view** of her face that matters. You ask no q**uestions of the purplish airbrush tones be**yond the lower Manhattan skyline, seen **from th**e deck of the bridge's first gothic tow**er; no docume ntation is required for yell**ow skyscraper lights or wooden-car rattl**e of Bro**oklyn-bound el trains. Later, with its n**ecessities, com es knowledge of the doing**s of newspaper barons, political bosses, p**rosecut**ing attorneys, architects and city plan**ners, reformer s, peddlers, pickpockets an**d public relations men. In the end, thoug**h, you** go back to the bridge at twilight, ba**ck to the bridge.**

"What's
the good
word from
Madison
Avenue?"

"Indefectible! That's the good
word. Incredible creativity.
Perspicacious! Ideas that are
ornaments of intellect...
layouts, merely consummate.
Sudler & Hennessey, obviously.
The observed of all observers,
the cynosure of all eyes, S & H
casually create incomparable
comprehensives, meticulous
mechanicals & fastidious
finishes. To say nothing of
apt art, felicitous photography
& resplendent retouching.
Typographic knowledge?
Encyclopaedic! Lettering?
Legendary! What's more their
reputation rests on reason,
practicality & pragmatism.
The good words from
Madison
Avenue?
Sudler &
Hennessey!"

"Who told you?"
"Father"*

50

imagination! **L'A**iglon *has it . . . have you?*

¡OLE! IS THE WILDLY ROMANTIC NEW SPANISH PURPLE WE PUT AT YOUR FEET FOR SPRING. EXACTLY WHAT HAPPENS WHEN YOU ADD A THROB OF THIS VIOLET SHOELEATHER TO BLACK AND WHITE COSTUMES? NAVY SUITS? GREYS, LILAC-Y BLUES, AZALEA PINKS? **OLE, OLE!** DO COME IN TO SEE THE FINEBONED PUMPS BY I. MILLER, 29.95 TO 32.95 AND THE MATCHED HANDBAGS STARTING AT 25.00* AT **I. MILLER**

D. LISNER & CO.

Party Lines: the waist cinching satin cummerbund, the camisole bodice, the great, full skirt of gentle chiffon . . . all looking ever so feminine when topped with the boyish bellhop jacket. Black or red with white skirt. Sizes 5 to 15. $35. Gernes Garment Company, 1407 Broadway, New York, N. Y.

Gay**G**ibson

Party lines: the waist cinching satin cummerbund, the camisole bodice, the great, full skirt of chiffon . . . all looking ever so feminine when topped with the boyish bellhop jersey jacket. Black or red with white skirt. Sizes 5 to 15. $35. Gernes Garment Company, 1407 Broadway, New York, N. Y.

Gay**G**ibson

imagination!

L'*A*IGLON HAS IT...HAVE YOU?

**Lawrence
of
London
creates
cosmopolitan
drama
with
Sag-no-mor®
jersey
by**

COMPANION
OF ALL YOUR DAYS,
RAIN OR SHINE.
IN THE LUXURY JERSEY
WYNER ENDOWS
WITH THE SUBTLE
MULTI-COLORS
OF THE EARTH.
ABOUT $80.

**Lawrence
of
London
creates
cosmopolitan
drama
with
Sag-no-mor®
jersey
by**

COMPANION
OF ALL YOUR DAYS
RAIN OR SHINE.
IN THE LUXURY JERSEY
WYNER ENDOWS
WITH THE SUBTLE
MULTI-COLORS
OF THE EARTH.
ABOUT $80.

Puccini
TOSCA
Milanov
Bjoerling
Warren

Rome Opera House
Orchestra and Chorus
Erich Leinsdorf,
Conductor

The Carita Salon at Henri Bendel

announces the opening of a

Late Edition Shop at 740 Madison Avenue

Here, in an annex to her Bendel Beauty Salon, Carita will specialize in
extraordinary services . . . from difficult hair-conditioning and
coloring, to pre-theatre comb-outs. There will be private keys for customers with
after-five appointments. And, your Bendel charge account will be
honored here, of course. Telephone LEhigh 5-6646 for appointments in
the Madison Avenue Shop . . . call CIrcle 7-1100 for appointments
in the Carita Salon at Henri Bendel, 10 West 57th Street

■ On Saturday, June 28th, we are moving into our own new building, brilliantly designed and engineered to help us provide faster, more efficient service to all our customers. For the first time all the fine Milliken products will be sold, serviced and administered from a single headquarters. ■

■ Carded Cotton Greige Goods
Combed Cotton Greige Goods
Filament Synthetic Greige Goods
Spun Synthetic Greige Goods
Nylon Tricot
Drapery Fabrics
Tire Cords
Wool, Wool Blends and Synthetic Finished Piece Goods
Stretch Nylon Yarn
Weaving and Knitting Yarns
Baby Products Division
Metal Insulating Fabrics
Deering Milliken Export Corporation

Deering-Milliken & Co. / Milliken Woolens, Inc. / 1045 Sixth Avenue, New York, N. Y. Phone: OXfo

all of us are

Moving

𝒜 ℳ

𝒜   𝒜

ℳ

ll Of

Us   re

oving

To the early Americans who settled in the original Atlantic seaboard colonies, and later, to the frontiersmen of the West, apples were important. Apples could be buried in the ground at Summer's end and hold until the Spring. They provided mincemeats, apple butter and apple cider, vinegar for pickles and preserves; and they could be bartered for eggs and potatoes. Every settler was mindful of apples and wanted a good plot of trees set out. ■ Johnny Appleseed, a bachelor from Massachusetts and Connecticut, knew this well. He sensed where western pioneers were likely to settle, got there ahead of time, planted some apple trees, then moved on to the next area of likely settlement. **THUS, HE INSTALLED A STRING OF NURSERIES OVER THE SCOPE OF THE FRONTIER, AND WHEN THE SETTLERS CAME, THE TREES WERE READY.**

AND THAT'S HOW JOHN CHAPMAN (JOHNNY'S REAL NAME) MADE HIS LIVING. In song and story, though, we see him preaching a holy gospel of apples, pleading with the settlers not to forget apples (for apples' sake) in the haste of clearing the land, hunting game, fighting Indians, building log cabins and getting in a crop. Because, as fabled Johnny put it **AROMATIC APPLE TREES IN SPRING BLOSSOM ARE THE NOBLEST OF GOD'S HANDIWORK, A NECESSITY FOR CHILDREN'S CLIMBING AS WELL AS LOVERS' TRYST.**

Besides being remembered for his apple trees, Johnny is revered as the Indian's friend. It is written that he lived in their encampments and often tipped them of impending raids. ■ As a nation, in those early days—and now the whole world knows it—we did not make peace with the Indians nor learn to live with them as John Chapman seems to have done. But then John was a wandering frontiersman without a homestead, a bachelor, and probably lonely a good deal of the time, and

your lips speak the last word in fashion

Only an Elizabeth Arden lipstick has such rich, creamy texture; is so lasting, so lustrous, so gentle to the lips. Only an Elizabeth Arden lipstick offers such a wealth of distinguished colors, all beautifully coordinated to the clothes you wear. Only an Elizabeth Arden lipstick comes to you in Click-Change, the refill case that saves tempers and money. One twist and the used lipstick clicks out. Another twist and the new lipstick clicks in. No scooping out. No squeezing in. No messy hands. New Click-Change lipstick, 1.75, Jewelled Case, 5.00. Refill, .85.

Cotton: born and bred for gentlemen

Cotton, so well bred for so many years, strikes a responsive chord in men of good breeding. One of the chief reasons is that cotton always keeps its word. It promises to wear well, to promote comfort, and to look fresh and personable after repeated washings. All these cotton does unfailingly. For example, you can be sure that this cool, interestingly woven leisure shirt by **Alfred of New York** in a new textured cotton by Everfast will continue to look as smart, as spanking white and as beautifully tailored until the very last day you wear it. You'll find it at fine stores throughout the country including Frank Bros., New York-Palm Beach; Stix Baer & Fuller, St. Louis; Kaufmann's, Pittsburgh; Dayton Co., Minneapolis; Julius Lewis, Memphis; Sy DeVore, Hollywood; Street's, Tulsa.

GARDEN IN THE SUN...

Glamor in the sun . . . in Jeanne d'Arc's enchanting sundress
of printed Dacron with its demure little cover jacket of rayon linen!
The dress to wash, drip-dry and forget about ironing! Yellow (shown), pink, blue.
Sizes 5 to 15. $22.95. At fine stores everywhere. For nearest store, write Dept. S,
Jeanne D'Arc *Division of L'Aiglon Apparel, Inc., 1350 Broadway, New York 18.*

Grand illusion–is it…or isn't it? You'll never guess so we'll tell you it's simply one of the many fine Borg deep pile fabrics that look like fur. You'll find these fabrics used as collars, cuffs, liners and even entire coats by the nation's best makers of outerwear. Fashions featuring Borg fabrics are always identified by the Borg label. Look for it.   a **B**org fabric

"Right now, I'd like to
get into a refrigerator
with 6 bottles of
Utica Club beer. I'd be a
cool mug. That's cat talk,
Dooley. Cool,
Crazy."

"Sometimes
I don't understand
you at all,
Schultz."

An Open Letter to Teachers

If the great New York Philharmonic Orchestra were going to play in your town tonight, would you urge the boys and girls in your class to attend? If the program said that Leonard Bernstein or Stokowski or Mitropoulos were going to conduct masterpieces of Beethoven or Mozart or Bartok, would you encourage your students to experience this important event? We feel that you would.

EVERY WEEK the New York Philharmonic does play in almost every town across America, over CBS Radio. No one has to stir from home. No one has to buy a ticket. A radio is your front seat.

This fine broadcast is just one of many programs on CBS Radio that make a deliberate effort to bring to your town cultural, informative, educational and, just as important, entertaining events that waken your students to new ideas and great occasions, that teach them that the arts are for enjoying, that learning is for living, and show them that the work you do in class extends far beyond the blackboards.

Every week your students can attend the concerts of the magnificent Cleveland Symphony under the direction of George Szell and Associate Conductor Robert Shaw. They can also enjoy a weekly performance of the Metropolitan Opera from New York City during its season. So many young people have learned over the years from these broadcasts that "Carmen" and "Faust" and "Madame Butterfly" are actually exciting stories; that opera singers, once appreciated, have as much to offer them as popular singers; that intermission features like Clifton Fadiman's interviews or Edward Downes' "Opera Quiz" are great fun. Have you given them an inkling of how fascinating such worthwhile programs are?

Has it occurred to you to tie in "The Hidden Revolution" series over CBS Radio with your discussions in current events and social sciences and government? Last year this series won the Peabody Award for outstanding public service. The subject is the changes, developments and political upheavals taking place in the world today. History before it's history! History while it's still a news story! Edward R. Murrow and Howard K. Smith narrate these programs. Your pupils will get to know men like Vice President Richard M. Nixon, playwright Archibald MacLeish, Dr. Clyde Kluckhohn, Professor of Anthropology at Harvard University.

Do your students know how fascinating news can be when they hear it from a man like Lowell Thomas over CBS Radio? He has been a cow puncher, gold miner, college professor, newspaper reporter, editor, historian, lecturer, author of more than 45 books. His gift is an incomparable one. By telling the big, important stories colorfully and concisely, he makes them real and memorable.

Have you alerted your class to the fact that twice each day they can travel to the remote corners of the globe and get the news first-hand from the finest news reporters in the world—the CBS News correspondents? The programs are "World News Roundup" and "The World Tonight." And top newsmen like Eric Sevareid, David Schoenbrun, Daniel Schorr and Winston Burdett tell the story directly from the scene.

In your classwork in government or history have you suggested that your students listen to "Capitol Cloakroom," and "The Leading Question," broadcast each week on the CBS Radio Network? They'll meet national leaders, get to know their personalities and attitudes, get familiar with important public affairs as they take shape. Fine learning tool for future statesmen!

Is your class aware that by listening to "Face The Nation" on CBS Radio they can hear, firsthand, opinions of leading world figures, as informed reporters question them? Great inspiration for future journalists, and voters!

Do your students know what they are missing by not hearing "Invitation To Learning"? Recently critic Alfred Kazin discussed Mark Twain's "Life on the Mississippi." Another week Perry Miller and Howard Mumford Jones of Harvard University discussed "A Tale of Two Cities." Every week a well-known authority gives a new breath of life to an important literary work on this exceptionally informative program.

DO YOU REALIZE how many CBS Radio programs are worthy of being made assignments for specific classroom discussion? Make it a habit to glance at your local daily radio schedules. For just to point out to the boys and girls who sit before you every day the fine opportunities they might be missing right in their own homes, just to hint that they might actually enjoy "Aïda" or Haydn's "Surprise" Symphony or a special news program might be opening a career, planting an ambition, enlarging life for them.

To miss such an opportunity to open young minds to what lies so close at hand, so eager for use, so ready to serve, so very worthwhile, might be to miss one of the great challenges of teaching. For what better way can we stir these young minds to think, to learn by doing, than by suggesting they use their time for something stimulating, something constructive, something that is theirs simply for the turning of a little knob.

If today radio stopped bringing such events to your town, if the New York Philharmonic no longer brought Beethoven, if "World News Roundup" no longer took you to Algiers and Tokyo, if the Metropolitan Opera performed only for New Yorkers, if intelligent worldwide news programs gave way to sensational headline flashes, if the only music available were the latest rock 'n' roll recordings, then you and your community would be striving to improve the quality of radio. Fortunately CBS Radio constantly strives to bring you educational, informative, cultural programs that assure your town the finest broadcasting fare.

IT IS YOU, by your listening, by your interest, who control the quality of programming brought to your students, the men and women of tomorrow. Suppose, by your lack of enthusiasm, all these wonderful things were no longer available, no longer waiting to be heard. Wouldn't you as a teacher make every effort to bring them back?—CBS Radio Network

INSIDE FASHION BY BORG! A FLASH OF COLOR WHEN YOUR COAT IS OPEN, A FLUSH OF WARMTH WHEN YOUR COAT IS CLOSED. BORG LINER,* ALWAYS SO LIGHT, SO LUSH, SO COMFORTING BRINGS NEW DRAMA AND UTILITY TO THE ALL-WEATHER COAT. MAKE SURE YOUR NEXT ALL-WEATHER COAT IS BORG LINED BY LOOKING FOR THE BORG LABEL.

A BORG FABRIC   **A M**ODELIA COAT

THE
GOLD
LOOK

Treasure, not buried, but gleaming gloriously at throat or wrist | as beautiful as the real thing! Designed and made with infinite care.
In textured make-believe gold | or silver. Bracelet, necklace, earrings, pin: each $2 plus tax.
At fine stores everywhere. | All designs copyright 1959 D. Lisner & Co., 393 Fifth Avenue, New York.

Tneasune!

Treasure!

dəəp

dəəp

dəəp

dəəp

dəəp

deep

deep

deep

deep

deep

deep

sleep

dead

Dacron and Cotton / Speaking of weather... this L'Aiglon slips from season to season with easy charm! Requires little or no ironing. Black-embroidered green (shown), brown or black. Sizes 8 to 20. $22.95

1.
Cotton / Tiny, varied-colored flowers glow like jewels on this dress that's neat enough for business, sweet enough for social doings—blooms beautifully all year 'round! Blue (shown), green, brown. Sizes 10 to 20. $17.95

2.
Dacron / Twice blessed: this L'Aiglon takes variable weather in stride, shines equally on coolish summer days, on all but the coldest winter days. To wash, drip dry, not iron! Brown (shown), green, blue. Sizes 8 to 20. $22.95

3.
Rayon and Cotton / Two-part story: the sweet-figured fashion that gives you a jacket when there's frost in the air, lets you shed it when the temperature soars! Hand washable. In black only. Sizes 8 to 20. $24.95

4.
Cotton / Perfection is another word for this shirtdress by L'Aiglon with its delicately cut convertible collar, its slim waistline, its gently bouffant skirt. Brown (shown), green, blue. Sizes 10 to 20. $19.95

5.
Imported Cotton / Inter-season traveler: the dress that commutes from summer to fall at the whim of the weather! Black lace at strategic points! Blue/black (shown); brown/black; lilac/black. Sizes 8 to 20. $22.95

6.
Dacron and Cotton / The fine art of being two places in the same outfit: in the office with the cropped jacket, at a party without! Requires little or no ironing! In brown plaid (shown); green or blue. Sizes 8 to 20. $24.95

1 ■ Sheer all wool costume, successful with or without jacket! Black (shown), red, olive. Sizes 10 to 20, 12½ to 20½. $29.95.

2 ■ Good as gold, the fashion of this all wool plaid! Brown/red (shown); charcoal/cognac; green/turquoise. Sizes 8 to 20. $24.95.

3 ■ Glen plaid shirtdress of 55% Zefran Acrylic, 45% Wool. Black/white (shown); brown/white; olive/white. Sizes 10 to 20. $24.95.

4 ■ Permanently pleated jersey of 80% Orlon Acrylic, 20% Wool! Coral (as shown), beige or blue. Sizes 10 to 20. $24.95.

5 ■ Collector's item: dress of 55% Dacron Polyester, 45% Rayon! Brown (shown), olive or charcoal. Sizes 10 to 20. $22.95.

6 ■ Work of art: sheath, with brass buttons! It's half Arnel Triacetate, half Rayon in brass (shown), blue or smoke. Sizes 8 to 20. $17.95.

Geigy Pharmaceuticals
Division of Geigy Chemical Corporation
P. O. Box 430, Yonkers, New York

Supply Request

to:

Dept. _____

Terr. No. _____

Date _____   Shipped Via _____   Prepaid _____

Quant.	Cont.	Size	Product Name and Form		Strength or Concen.	Quant.	Cont.	Size	Product Name and Form		Strength or Concen.
	Vial	15	**Preludin**	Tablets	25 mg.		Bottle	25	**Tromexan**	Tablets	300 mg.
	Vial	6	**Preludin Endurets**	Tablets	75 mg.		Bottle	50	**Sintrom**	Tablets	4 mg.
	Vial	12	**Butazolidin**	Tablets	100 mg.		Vial	12	**Sterazolidin**	Capsules	50 mg.- 1.25 mg.
	Vial	12	**Butazolidin alka**	Capsules	100 mg.		Vial	30	**Anturan**	Tablets	100 mg.
	Catch Cover	6	**Dulcolax**	Tablets	5 mg.		Catch Cover	15	**Tofränil**	Tablets	25 mg.
	Box	2	**Dulcolax**	Suppositories	10 mg.		Amp.	10	**Tofränil**	Solution	25 mg./ 2 cc
	Tube	5 gm	**Eurax**	Cream	10%						
	Bottle	12 cc	**Eurax**	Lotion	10%						
	Tube	5 gm	**Sterosan**	Cream	3%						
	Tube	5 gm	**Sterosan**	Ointment	3%						
	Tube	5 gm	**Sterosan— hydrocortisone**	Cream	3% -1%						
	Tube	5 gm	**Sterosan— hydrocortisone**	Ointment	3% -1%						
	Vial	6	**Medomin**	Tablets	200 mg.						
	Bottle	100	**Panparnit**	Tablets	12.5 mg.						

☐ Business Reply Card Sample

☐ Convention Sample Follow-up

☐ Literature

☐

Date Shipped _____

Packed By _____

Weight _____

B/L No. _____

Credit _____

Debit _____

Budget Appr. _____

Postage _____

Special Delivery _____

Insurance _____

Total _____

Geigy Pharmaceuticals
P. O. Box 430
Yonkers, New York

Requested By _____

Approved By _____

Packing Slip

CLIENT_____ DESCRIPTION_____

_____

_____

DATE_____ JOB NO._____ ESTIMATE BY_____

QUANTITY_____ NO. OF PAGES_____ STOCK_____

SIZE_____ COLORS_____ BINDING_____

ART COSTS				PRODUCTION COSTS
LAYOUT				TYPOGRAPHY
ROUGHS				SCREEN VELOXES
COMPS				COPY PRINTS
TYPE LAYOUT & SPEC.				ENGRAVING
FINISHED ART				ELECTROS
LETTERING				MATS
PHOTOGRAPHY				PRINTING
RETOUCHING				STOCK
MODEL FEES				BINDERY
SPECIAL PROPS				ENVELOPES
MECHANICAL PASTE UP				POSTAGE
PHOTOSTATS				SHIPPING COST
MISCELLANEOUS				MISCELLANEOUS
				SUB TOTAL ART & PRODUCTION
				AGENCY COMMISSION
				SALES TAX
				TOTAL

ADDITIONAL INFORMATION_____

_____

_____

CLIENT APPROVAL_____ ACCOUNT EXECUTIVE APPROVAL_____

25/This is an example of optical flush-left alignment. The Lightline Gothic lines are aligned flush with the lower-left edge of the large "W." Note that the second and third lines beginning with the letters "W" and "A" have been set slightly further to the left because of the diagonal indent of those letters while the fifth line, which begins with the letter "T," has not been moved to the left because of the two vertically stroked letters above and beneath it. Normally the letter "T" should be set with a compensation made for the overhanging top stroke.

Observe how close the lines are to each other. This is possible because the typeface used is a Title Gothic. Title Gothics have no lower case and because of this can be cast on the full height of the point size. The typeface used in this example is 12 pt Lightline Title Gothic. It is the exact height, width, and weight of 14 pt Lightline Gothic. Because Lightline Gothic has a lower-case alphabet, its capital letters are smaller than Lightline Title Gothic, exactly a full size smaller.

The large capital "W" was set in Railroad Gothic, another all-capital font, which made it possible to set the first line as close as it is.

The lesson to remember from this example is that whenever the design calls for lines to be set very close to each other, always specify a typeface with an all-capital font.

w: 96 pt Railroad Gothic
TEXT: 12 pt Lightline Title Gothic

26/This self-advertisement was designed to impress the reader with the creative use of copy and typography. By omitting the letter spacing between the "I" and the "Q," the interesting "IQ" design element was formed.

The text matter has been set with very close word spacing and the periods at the extreme right edge of the copy have been "hung" in the margin. If the periods had been set flush right, mechanically, there would have been optical "holes" at the ends of these lines. The spacing between words in the first line is an excellent example of "tight" word spacing. Notice that the lengths of the words used in lines 2 and 4 create a different textural appearance compared to those used in lines 3 and 7. The lengths of words will very often affect the texture of body text.

HEADLINE: 36 pt Bookman Old Style Italic, No. 981
TEXT: 18 pt New Bookman (Hess), No. 398

27/The type for this page was first set normally, and then photographically curved to achieve the "SWELLING" effect that we see. The idea was to make the reader want to "flatten" the page. The sensual experience that the reader received was exactly what the designer wanted. The purpose of the design was to cause the reader to pause for a moment, long enough, perhaps, to read the message or remember the name of the product and its function.

Notice how close the letters are in the word "SWELLING." They actually touch in some instances. Notice also how other letters in the headline appear to be set much closer than is possible in typesetting. The designer of this page used a razor blade on the type proofs in order to bring the letters closer together and so achieve the "tight" feeling that he wanted.

A closer look at the third, fourth and fifth lines of the body text will reveal that the word "DIMETANE" was set in caps, one size smaller than the body text, rather than in small caps of the body text. Small capitals were not used in this instance because there are no small-cap numerals in this font and, on the last line of the text, the word "DIMETANE" is followed by the figure 100. The selection of type was made with this in mind, so that the figure 100 would not appear larger than the word "DIMETANE."

CASLON NO. 540 Series (Photographically Curved)
SWELLING: Hand Lettering (Photographically Curved)

28-29/An example of figurative typography in reverse. Figurative typography is typography that has been shaped to represent the form of an object. Had this typography been set in the shape of the car, rather than set around the car, we would have had a typical example of figurative typography.

In this instance the layout was submitted to the typographer with a photostat of the automobile pasted in position, and with lines drawn to indicate the shape desired around the car.

In all cases of figurative typography it is necessary for the leading, or space between lines, to be pre-specified. Herein lies the danger. If the shape does not fit perfectly on the first setting, resetting and sometimes two or three resettings will be necessary. The typesetter must measure and count the number of lines against the layout, as he is setting, in order to achieve the shape desired.

Note that all paragraphs are flush left. There are no indentions. Each paragraph indication is gained from a "widow," the short last line of the preceding paragraph. This special treatment was done to keep an evenness of color on the page, so as not to interfere with the figurative typography.

In the lower right column observe the use of small capitals for the names of the states, and the use of diagonal slashes (shilling marks) to separate units from each other. This was a particularly difficult block of copy to handle because there were so many figures, colons, commas, and periods in the text. The over-all appearance of this block has an evenness of color that is very pleasing and harmonious with the rest of the page. This section, badly handled, could have seriously affected the aesthetic beauty of the entire page.

ROVER: Hand Lettering
TEXT: 9 pt Garamond (Intertype) 1 pt leaded
ITALIC PARAGRAPH: 14 Garamond Italic (Intertype), 2 pt leaded

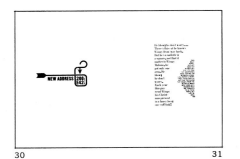

30

31

30 / This "moving" announcement was created out of miscellaneous type characters and composed as one unit. The reader is cautioned against making this a practice if cost is a factor. It is much cheaper to paste it all together. But a busy art director's time is more costly than a compositor's time and he is often more than justified in ordering complete makeup such as this.

The optical disturbances that pasteup edges create often interfere with the easy grasp of a complete unit of typography. In such instances, makeup by the compositor more than compensates for the expense.

When it is necessary to paste together several units of typography, it is wise to make an accurate tracing of the completed pasteup in order to see the entire page without pasteup marks. This is time-consuming and painstaking work but it should be done—if there is time and if you care enough about the job you are doing.

30 pt Railroad Gothic with 10 pt Standard Regular

31 / Another example of figurative typography. The use of the bold punctuation marks, taken from type-faces of totally different character and style, is a most unusual treatment.

Note also the "hung" punctuation marks on the small Lightline Gothic caps in order to achieve an optical alignment on the right edge. This is in addition to the bold exclamation mark which is hung purposely in the margin for emphasis.

BOLD FACE: 24 pt Small Torino with Ultra Bodoni Punctuation Marks
LIGHT FACE: 10 pt Lightline Gothic with Franklin Gothic Punctuation Marks

32

33

32 / This vertical block of copy is an excellent exam-ple of the problems that beset the typographer-designer when specifying a block of type with a measure to be justified at both the left and right edges.

A first glance at the column gives one an over-all impression of evenness of color, which, after all, is the main purpose. However, had this copy been a group of only six or seven lines, the glaring imper-fections would be too noticeable to be tolerated. Study the lines individually and you will be able to find many examples of poorly set lines; lines that have more letter spacing and word spacing than others because of the restrictions and limitations that accompany such a flush-left and flush-right specification.

The designer accepted the imperfect typography because of the over-all color that such a vertical rectangular column of typography created. Had better typography been desired, a flush edge at the left with a ragged edge at the right would have been specified. This would have permitted the type-setter to use the same amount of space between all words and would have achieved uniform color throughout all lines.

8 pt Franklin Gothic Italic, 2 pt leaded

33 / Observe in the last line of this paragraph the use of a bold exclamation point and the failure to hang the final period in the right margin. Notice therefore how the last line appears to be slightly shorter than the lines above it.

Compare the apostrophe and question mark that appear in the bold words "ugh!'ly." Very often such subtle points will influence the designer in his choice of type. It is good practice to become con-scious of the punctuation marks in the alphabet of the type that you are using as well as the style of the figures.

UGH!'LY?: 120 pt Franklin Gothic Extra Condensed also 48 pt Grotesque No. 9
TEXT: 18 pt Lightline Gothic, 3 pt leaded with 18 pt Grotesque No. 9 for bold face

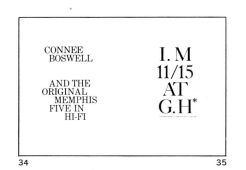

34

35

34-35 / The example on page 34 shows a pleasing arrangement of an all-capital setting. An otherwise ordinary setting of lines was made very interesting by juggling the lines slightly off the center axis.

On page 35 notice the use of the slash mark on the second line between the figures 11 and 15. Al-though the example shown here is with a bold slash, this advertisement actually appeared in print with a hairline slash. It is not easy to imagine the change that such a thin line would make, but if you draw a hairline rule on a piece of paper and lay it over the bold one you will really see what eventually appeared.

There is no rule that one must use an unattractive mark of punctuation just because it comes in the font of type one is using. There are hundreds of typeface fonts that contain one or two weak

characters. It is up to the student of typography to learn to recognize these weaknesses and to compen-sate for them by redrawing weak letters or borrow-ing from a different font.

PAGE 34: 60 pt Century Expanded
PAGE 35: 120 pt Caslon 540; 10 pt Bodoni Italic

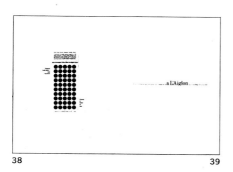

36-37 / On this spread two typefaces have been used that are completely different in character and style. One a light sans serif; the other a bold black face. However, when one reads the text and realizes that the subject matter has to do with "overeating," the choice of typefaces seems perfect.

There are many faces, such as the bold Cooper Black, that lie unused in the typecases of composing rooms all over the world. These faces are occasionally revived by contemporary designers who overlook their dated nature because they present an opportunity for contemporary solutions to current typographic problems.

On page 37, note that the word "Ambar" at the bottom of the centered column is not centered optically; it is too far to the left. It should be moved 2 or 3 points to the right to allow for the small trademark sign.

PAGE 36: 36 pt Cooper Black
PAGE 37: 18 pt Lightline Gothic with
18 pt Cooper Black

36   37

38 / The large circular bullets are set in type and the ruled box encloses the entire form. One must be aware when ordering butting type rules that it is impossible for all corners to touch. Therefore "touching up" is necessary when the type is used for camera reproduction.

Notice that the text at the top begins with quotes on the first line. Observe that the mechanical alignment of the quotes at the left creates an optical indent in that paragraph. One might think that this would have looked more pleasing had the quotes been hung in the left margin. Although this might have been more pleasing, one must question what would have happened to the word spacing in that line if such a refinement had been made. It would have been necessary either to increase the space between words or to bring up part of the first word of the second line. This is always a problem and very often, in cases such as this, decisions are made that seem to contradict "refinement" principles.

30 pt Bullets
10 pt Cooper Black
6 pt No. 4, 8 pt and 10 pt Lightline Gothic

39 / This is a combination of two linotype slugs separated by foundry (handset) type.

Notice that the last five words at the end of the line drop slightly below the alignment of the hand type to its left. This is always the danger when types of different point sizes are forced to justify with each other. In order to understand and anticipate this kind of problem, one must try to visualize the metal as it actually is. Here the size of type for "L'Aiglon" is larger than the linotype slugs. As a result the compositor had to "build up" on both sides of the hand type to fit the two slugs on a horizontal alignment at the bottom. Obviously, something went wrong in the placement of metal space on the right edge and this misalignment is the result. The designer, however, did not accept this first proof. The reader should try to recall whether he noticed this before it was brought to his attention.

12 pt Underwood Typewriter
36 pt Torino

38   39

---

40 / This page was part of a planned advertisement for an airline company.

The use of different typefaces for the cities gave a foreign look to the advertisement, and the symmetrical layout permitted each line to stand out by itself.

The large "A" at the top and "Z" at the bottom were all part of the copy-design—to illustrate effectively the idea of "all this, from A to Z . . . and Ireland, too." Note also the delicate use of hairline rules to separate the cities.

A-Z: 120 pt Franklin Gothic Extra Condensed
AMSTERDAM: 24 pt Railroad Gothic
BARCELONA: 30 pt Century Bold Condensed
BIRMINGHAM: 30 pt Ultra Bodoni Extra Condensed
BLACKPOOL: 30 pt News Gothic Condensed
BRISTOL: 30 pt Bodoni Book
BRUSSELS: 30 pt Cloister Black
CARDIFF: 30 pt Times Roman
COPENHAGEN: 24 pt Cooper Black
DUSSELDORF: 24 pt Peignot Bold
EDINBURGH: 24 pt Jim Crow
FRANKFORT: 30 pt Cloister Black
GLASGOW: 30 pt Ultra Bodoni Extra Condensed
LISBON: 30 pt Alternate Gothic No. 1
LIVERPOOL: 30 pt Century Bold Condensed
LONDON: 24 pt No. 30 Heavy Copperplate Gothic
LOURDES: 30 pt Baskerville

MANCHESTER: 30 pt News Gothic Condensed
NEWCASTLE-ON-TYNE: 24 pt Extra Condensed
Title Gothic No. 12
PARIS: 30 pt Astoria
ROME: 30 pt Bauer Bodoni
ZURICH: 24 pt Railroad Gothic
ALL THIS . . . AND IRELAND, TOO!: 24 pt Century
Expanded Italic

41 / In this example the name of the client has been treated illustratively and integrated as a logotype into the text.

The cap "L" is of a completely different typeface and size. The size was chosen with the idea of having the bottom stroke of the "L" align optically (but slightly larger) with the height of the italic lines.

Note also the interesting stagger of the text lines, which are divided almost centrally by the vertical stroke of the cap "L."

TEXT: 10 pt De Vinne Italic, 6 pt leaded
L: 54 pt Venus Bold Extended
ISNER: 12 pt Venus Bold Extended

40   41

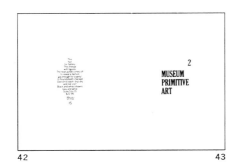

42/The lines on this page are all centered and set solid (no leading between lines). Note that the underscores are handled with hairline rules, not with rules that are the same weight as the typeface used.

Had underscores similar to the weight of the typeface been used, they would not have provided contrast; they would have merely clogged up the space between the copy and the rule.

In this instance the bottom of the type had to be shaved off in order to bring the hairline rules as close as they are.

In photo lithography, rules can be drawn in on the type proof. In letterpress printing, the rules must be set in the form.

TEXT: 18 pt Lightline Gothic, set solid
THIS IS: 36 pt Lightline Gothic

43/The combination of a small, light, sans serif capital letter with a large, bold, condensed serif face has formed a beautiful composition. The subtleties abound all about these lines.

Notice the vertical and horizontal alignments of the words "THE" and "OF" as well as the optical flush alignment of the three bold words.

60 pt Cheltenham Bold Extra Condensed
14 pt Standard Light

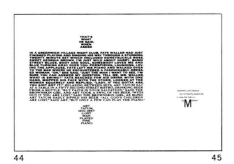

44-45/On the left we see a setting of experimental typography. The combination of two bold faces, one sans serif and one serif face might cause raised eyebrows; this treatment, however, is appropriate for the copy—part of an article on Jazz. The effect was heightened in the final presentation by the use of color. The bold sans serif was printed in red and the bold serif face printed in blue.

Here we also see an excellent example of "hung" punctuation marks on the extreme right edge of the text. Notice particularly the bottom line in which

both the period and final quotation marks are hung beyond the text area.

The copy on the right of page 45 is another example of the blending of two typefaces, in which a bold face is chosen to fit the character of the light face and integrated into a pleasing solution.

PAGE 44: 18 pt Franklin Gothic Wide
18 pt Cheltenham Bold Extended
PAGE 45: 18 pt Lightline Gothic
M: 72 pt News Gothic

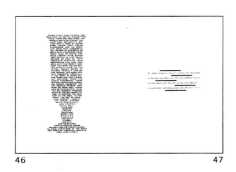

46/Another example of figurative typography. Once again the reader can observe the rivers of white space that flow vertically through the text and the poorly set lines with either too much or too little word spacing. This is the penalty for such setting. However this is very often overlooked in favor of the ultimate result. As in this instance, one has to decide whether the over-all effect does or does not justify the disadvantages of such settings.

10 pt Gothic No. 25 (Linotype)

47/A most unusual handling of rules. The four lines of italic are flush left and flush right while the bold horizontal rules dance freely left and right. Even though the bars are shown in black, one can easily imagine them in five different colors as the first two words of the text suggest.

12 pt Scotch Italic (Linotype) with 6 pt Rules

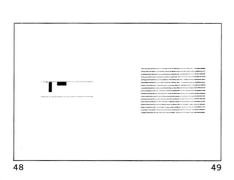

48/Part of a page for an experimental project in typography. The use of thick rules to the width of the emphasized words is a most unusual and effective handling of underscores. These two lines actually appeared in print as one long line, centered underneath a large black-and-white photograph of an elevated subway system that is in the process of being dismantled. The tall beams in the photograph, which stand so erect in defiance of their destruction, are dramatically enhanced by the exciting use of such underscores.

6 pt Standard Light Condensed

49/This page is not shown as an example of any recommended form of typography, but merely as an unusual solution to a problem.

The typefaces change abruptly every so many picas, even in the middle of words. This particular text was part of an article on New York City and the purpose of this exercise was to express the continually changing character of this city.

LEFT TO RIGHT:
6 pt Franklin Gothic
6 pt Bulmer
6 pt Latin Wide
6 pt No. 4 Lightline Gothic
6 pt Ultra Bodoni

50/The combination of an outline face with bold, solid punctuation marks of the same family creates a most unusual and interesting effect. This is another example of exciting typography which developed very simply out of an imaginative use of type elements. No distortions were necessary, the result—dynamic contrasts.

24 pt Cheltenham Bold Outline (Ludlow) with
24 pt Cheltenham Bold

51/Once again, the interesting use of large, bold initials of a different typeface integrated into a line of type. The particular point of interest here is the use of a different font for the serif apostrophe between the large sans-serif bold face. The use of three unrelated typefaces might defy all accepted laws but they also create a very interesting and pleasing unit of color.

14 pt Scotch Roman Italic, No. 361
96 pt Franklin Gothic Extra Condensed Initials with
Ultra Bodoni apostrophe

50   51

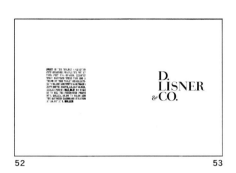

52/On this page we have another example similar to that on page 50. However in this instance the outline letters are all capitals. There is no solid "filled in" member of the family available, therefore it was necessary to choose a bold, solid typeface that resembled in character the outline counterpart.

While one may question the readability of outline typefaces in such quantity, one can hardly question the interesting effect of such treatment.

18 pt Outline Gothic No. 61 with
18 pt Railroad Gothic

53/The flush-left arrangement of the three lines (with the ampersand hung in the left margin) is a pleasing arrangement in itself. However, one receives a delightful experience upon observing that the period on the first line centers over the capital "I" in the second line. This may have been accidental or intentional; it does not matter— it is interesting nonetheless.

72 pt Bauer Bodoni Title
42 pt ampersand

52   53

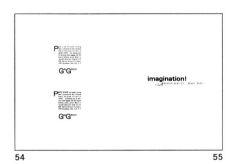

54/These two blocks of copy appear to be almost identical. However, note the difference in the visual appearance of each block when the initial cap "P" is followed by the same size body text in one instance and an enlarged size of the same text in another. Inasmuch as they are both interesting, this becomes another example of more than one solution to the same problem.

Also to be brought to the attention of the reader are the two words "Gay Gibson." In the bottom setting of these words note that the lower-case letters "ay" and "ibson" are aligned lower and slightly closer to the capitals than they appear in the top setting. This was a refinement made on the second revise.

TEXT: 12 pt Standard Light, 3 pt leaded with
24 pt Standard Light and 48 Standard Initials

55/This is another instance of assembling different typefaces into interestingly integrated units. The use of the large swash capital "A" and the alignment of the capital "L" and the apostrophe at the bottom of the swash was a subtle touch that turned an ordinary piece of typography into a pleasing arrangement.

IMAGINATION: 48 pt Gothic No. 545
L'AIGLON HAS: 18 pt Janson No. 401 with
36 pt Janson Italic Initial

54   55

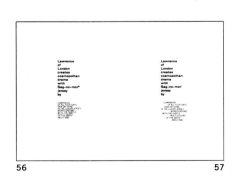

56-57/These two pages are a before-and-after treatment of the same copy. On page 56 the "tight" all-cap, sans serif copy has been set flush left with no leading.

On page 57 the lines have been leaded and staggered left and right to form an interesting shape. Notice how the eye follows down and around the outer extremities of the lines, never really invading the indented areas of space. The extra leading has been inserted to give the staggered lines room to "float" more comfortably. Observe also that the register mark after "sag-no-mor" has been set two sizes smaller.

This is not the only possible solution to this layout. Make a tracing of each line on separate pieces

of tracing paper. Lay the tracings down one on top of the other and then begin to move them back and forth. This "playing" with type, while time-consuming at first, is more than compensated for by the reward: seeing a pleasing shape develop under one's control. When you have everything exactly as you like it, Scotch tape or staple all the overlays together. Then make one final sketch for the typographer so that he cannot misinterpret your solution. It is more than worth all the effort.

(When you find yourself using this technique as a matter of habit, you can be sure that you are becoming professional.)

BOLD TYPE: 24 pt Gothic No. 545
LIGHT FACE: 12 pt Lightline Title Gothic

56   57

58/At first glance it might be difficult to find the one point of interest that ties all the lines on this page together. The reader might think of the thin horizontal rule as the separating element of interest. However it is the use of all capital letters in the word "TOSCA" that establishes the change of pace and interest for these lines. It is questionable whether this would have been as effective a piece of typography had the word "TOSCA" been in upper and lower case, even one or two sizes larger.

24, 48 and 72 pt Caslon 540

59/This is another example of symmetry. The sensitive use of three lines of script centered over seven lines of a roman typeface is a most pleasing combination and arrangement of typefaces.

Note also the figures in the bottom three lines of the text. These are called "lining figures"; they align optically, top and bottom, on the capital letters of that font. Old-style figures have no alignment and extend above and beneath the "x" height of the font.

PAGE 59: 20 pt Excelsior Script Semi Bold with 10 pt Garamond (Intertype), 5 pt leaded

---

60-61/This is from an actual reproduction proof that had all elements appearing in the exact positions shown here. The galley setting of swash letters and parts of words, shown on page 61, was done to give the designer a variety of letters in different sizes from which he could choose those he wished to piece together to form the headline. (Because complete ranges of swash letters are often no longer available, it is sometimes necessary for the designer to assemble words by enlarging or reducing characters that are available.)

The two blocks of copy are distinguished chiefly by the use of the black squares. At first glance one might think that the long signature line with the bold rule beneath it was shaved at the bottom in order to permit the rule to come as close as it does. However, look at the first word in the line and notice the lower case "g." The point to remember is that among the typefaces that have long and short descenders, some, such as this one, permit bars to be placed as close as the one we see here, others do not.

TEXT: 12 pt Caslon 471 (Linotype)
SIGNATURE LINE: 14 pt Caslon 540 (Linotype)
HEADLINE: 30 and 60 pt Franklin Gothic Italic and 72 pt Caslon Italic
INITIALS: Caslon Italic 540 and 471 Swash Initials

62/The interesting point to be observed on this page is the combination of two different typefaces, one all in caps, the other in upper and lower case, but both integrated into the same message. The effect produced gives the change of pace and emphasis desired.

When printed, all the bold capital letters appeared in blue and the light, sans serif, upper and lower case copy in red.

14 pt Lightline Gothic upper and lower case
12 pt Gothic No. 520 caps

63/This page appears to have two headlines. The signature "Elizabeth Arden" is so strongly stylized that the eye seems to focus upon it first. It was obvious to the designer, therefore, that the headline had to be one of contrast. This created another problem since a bold typeface, no matter what size

used, might have conflicted with the boldness of "Elizabeth Arden." The decision to use a large, light, sans serif typeface centered closely over the two columns of text created an over-all symmetrical appearance of dignity, and yet one that had within it three degrees of type texture, light—gray—dark.

In choosing type for headlines a good point to remember is "the larger the point size...the lighter the weight of the typeface" and "the smaller the point size . . . the bolder the typeface." This is a basic principle of contrast.

However, the reader must always take "space" into consideration. A small typeface must be smaller still if the space it is to appear in is a small one. We can also compensate with the use of color or screening of type, to control the "weight" of type.

HEAD: 36 pt Lightline Gothic
TEXT: 10 pt DeVinne (Linotype) 2 pt leaded

64/Notice the optical misalignments at the extreme right of both columns. Observe that the punctuation marks have all been flushed mechanically at the right edge, and that the eye seems to dance in and out along these edges. This example is shown as a comparison to other pages in this book wherein this lack of refinement has been corrected.

However, in spite of this, the over-all strength of this composition is sufficient to make the reader overlook the right edges of these columns. This can be attributed chiefly to the excellent spacing between words throughout the text, the use of the bold rule underneath the headline and the use of the bold type in the text at the bottom of the first column. These three elements draw one's attention away from the weaknesses elsewhere in the typography.

TEXT: 10 pt Lightline Gothic with 10 pt News Gothic Bold (Intertype)
HEAD: 18 pt Times Roman

65/In addition to the very interesting staggered arrangement of italic lines there are several points of interest to be brought to the attention of the reader.

Observe that the old-style figures in the body text have not been set in italic as is the rest of the text but have been kept in roman. In the second line from the bottom, notice that the designer has used a bolder and larger price-setting. This adds additional color to the typography.

The use of the bold Egyptian face for "Jeanne D'Arc" is interrupted delightfully by the use of a script letter for the capital "D."

GARDEN IN THE SUN: 24 pt Standard Light
TEXT: 12 pt Caslon 471 Italic (Linotype) with $22.95 in 18 pt, same face
JEANNE D'ARC: 20 pt Clarendon Bold with 14 pt Bank Script

66 / The use of the two large bold letters at the beginning and end of the block of text adds interest to four simple lines of text. The stickup initial on the first line and the drop initial on the last three words are further subtleties that add to this unusual treatment.

18 pt Lightline Gothic with
24 pt Franklin Gothic Wide Initials

67 / In this instance almost any typeface probably would have been effective. The copy is so humorous and so alive that the designer chose to use a typeface that was as unsophisticated as possible rather than a formal face with fine serifs or thin lines.

The staggered arrangement of these lines did little to affect the strong impact of the message. Once again, form is a result of content—and here we have an excellent example of "quality" content.

24 and 36 pt Cheltenham Medium

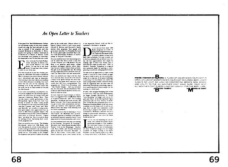

68 / This is similar to the example on page 69 in only one respect: the use of large and bold initials as ornamental elements.

Notice that the first two or three words of text that follow the large initials are all in small caps. This is considered good practice because the small caps align horizontally with the top of the large initial letters and allow the eye to flow gently into the text. This is particularly well-illustrated in the paragraph with the large cap "I." In the paragraphs with the caps "E" and "D" this has not been done properly and the space between the large initial and the first word of text is incorrect. All three initials were set in place mechanically. However it is only coincidental that the mechanical setting of the cap "I" happens to look well optically. Also notice that all paragraphs are set flush left. Therefore, in order to separate them, extra space has been added between each paragraph.

Notice that while the headline is not very large in its point size it appears much larger than it is because of the large panel of white space it is centered in.

TEXT: 11 pt Baskerville, 3 pt leaded with Baskerville initials
HEADLINE: 36 pt Bulmer Italic

69 / A text set in all caps need not be uninteresting nor need it be difficult to read. The judicious use of different weights of capital letters breaks up the monotony of grayness, and the use of large initials adds the sparkle that makes this an exciting page to look at.

TEXT: 10 pt Gothic No. 26 (Linotype) with Bold face in 10 pt Gothic No. 25 (Linotype)
LARGE INITIALS: 36 pt Gothic No. 545

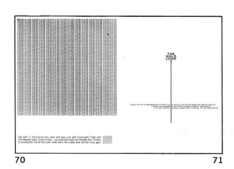

70 / This is another example of an over-all pattern of typography created by repeating lines of type one beneath the other. The shape of a large cap "C" was eventually cut out of this "wallpaper" effect and what remained was interesting in itself because of the beautiful repetition of letter forms.

COURTAULDS: 10 pt Gothic No. 26 (Linotype)
TEXT: 18 pt Lightline Gothic with "C's" in 6 pt News Gothic

71 / The placement of a long, vertical, bold arrow pointing upwards to the headline and separating the text, is most unusual. However, one cannot question its effectiveness.

The perfectionist might successfully argue the fact that the copy has been broken and readability impaired. The author suggests that the reader study these lines to determine whether the intrusion of the vertical bar is overly offensive or worth the slight loss in readability.

HEAD: 18 pt Gothic No. 520
TEXT: 10 pt Lightline Gothic, 2 pt leaded

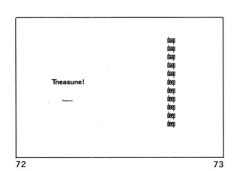

72 / Many typefaces have within them certain characters that are unpleasing, offensive, or not in keeping with the character of the rest of the letters in the font.

Observe, for instance, the small setting of the word "treasure" and you will notice that the lower case "r" looks both squashed and condensed and therefore is not in keeping with the rest of the letters. The designer, dissatisfied with this incongruity, solved this problem very cleverly.

He set the word "treasure" in the large size shown on this page but replaced the letters "r" with the letters "n." By painting out the lower-right part of the strokes of the "n," the designer created a lower case "r" that was in complete character with the rest of the letters.

This should indicate to the reader the possibility of resorting to similar solutions whenever certain letters prove aesthetically disturbing.

14 and 48 pt Gothic No. 545

73 / This is a very interesting and delightful experience. At first glance it appears as if the word "deep" has been set vertically eleven times. But, we are quite startled when we realize that this is not so. This page was composed by taking two proofs, turning one of them upside down and then joining both together. The fact that the lower case "d" turned upside down appears as a lower case "p" momentarily misleads the eye. It is only after closer observation that we notice that the "e's" at the top of the page have also been turned upside down.

60 pt News Gothic Extra Condensed

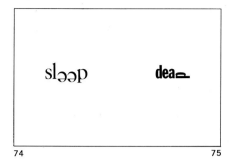

74   75

74-75 / These two pages are examples of experimental typography dealing with typographic "sound," "pattern," and "motion." An attempt has been made to make the words look like what they infer. The inverting of the two lower case "e's" to indicate drooping eyes and the "flopping" of the "d" in "dead" were interesting solutions. These little typographic exercises stimulate the mind; while they cannot be called typography as such, they are delightful exercises in typographic illustration.

SLEEP: Caslon 540 (enlarged)
DEAD: 120 pt Franklin Gothic Extra Condensed

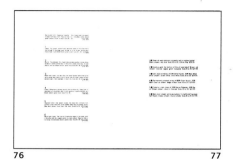

76   77

76-77 / These pages should be looked at together. They were designed by the same designer, and it is interesting to note how similar problems were solved for different occasions.

On page 76 you will notice that the key numbers of identity are flush left above the text and the price listings are flush right at the bottom of the text. Observe also that the dollar sign in front of the price listing is the size of the body text, and blends most effectively.

On page 77 the key figures are followed by a black square which creates the element of interest. Observe also that the price for the products is now in the same size as the text and the dollar sign is also in the same size.

PAGE 76, TEXT: 10 pt Standard Light, 2 pt leaded
NUMERALS: 18 pt Standard Light
PAGE 77: 12 pt Lightline Gothic

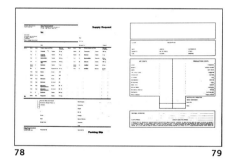

78   79

78-79 / These are beautiful examples of "order form" settings. On page 78 the entire form has been designed with vertical and horizontal alignments. It is only necessary to look at the left edge of the copy to be sure that it is virtually consistent throughout. A point of interest is that on both pages the vertical rules were overprinted at the typography shop. Normally either the horizontal or vertical rules would be drawn in. Another solution would be to have

the vertical or horizontal rules all set in position and butted. However, the butting of rules creates slight optical air spaces that mar the beauty of clean ruled work. Even though this may be objectionable, the difference in expense is apt to be the deciding factor.

PAGE 78: Standard with Standard Medium
PAGE 79: Lightline Gothic

suggested working habits for the student There are certain rules regarding working habits that are almost mandatory for good professional results. Some of them are as follows:

1. Get into the habit of thinking seriously about the type-written copy that you have in your hand; learn to examine the words themselves in order to find some key that will guide you to a solution of the problem.

The kind of words used and the style of writing can change the visual appearance of the text.

Although six-letter words such as "mammal" and "little" look and set the same when typed on a typewriter, they do not look or set the same in type. One is long and "smooth" because of the softness of the three rounded "m's" but the word "little" is made up of five straight verticals in a row thus producing a very sharp and condensed appearance.

The text of a writer who uses a predominance of short words will always have many more word spaces than a text with long words. This creates unevenness in color and texture; it also increases the danger of having rivers of white space run vertically through the text.

Therefore, get into the habit of reading or studying your copy; first, to know what you are setting and second, to try and spot any peculiarities in the style of writing. Such factors will probably affect your planning at the layout stage since your choice of column width and typeface may be influenced by the kind of text you are dealing with. (You would certainly think twice about setting a short choppy-looking text in a condensed typeface, which would only accentuate the choppiness. The selection of a rounded or extended face might be the wise choice because it would stretch out the short words, thereby breaking up the spottiness and lessening the chance of "rivers." This is not a rule—it is only a suggestion.)

Stop saying to yourself that you will juggle all the type in later. The time to do the planning is in the first layout stage, allowing enough margin and room for all type to fit in safely and fairly accurately. What good is a layout in which the subhead has been indicated to appear at the top of the page when it actually will fall, when set in type, in the middle of the page? The pleasing color and balance you indicated in your layout is now gone; as a result everything else will look different on the page. This certainly cannot be called planned typography.

Therefore, learn to work backwards. Know the time problem and mechanical requirements before you begin.

Know all the elements to be included: headlines, subheads, text, illustrations, logotypes, testimonials, order forms, and so forth. Have the illustrative matter beforehand. Know the actual wording of heads.

Evaluate your elements. Eliminate everything that isn't absolutely necessary. Simplify, simplify, simplify.

Then make a rough layout for yourself, plotting areas of space for type and illustration by allowing the space your trained eye estimates to be necessary for the paragraph, subheads and so forth. (In planning the layout great effort should be taken to strive for the simplest kind of format possible. Remember, the ultimate purpose of typography is to be read—and to be read, it must first be inviting.)

Then cast* out the longest paragraph in the typewritten text to determine the point size of type and amount of leading. This step will give you a measurement guide and will also give you a better picture of how much area you actually will need. Perhaps you will have to go wider on your column width, increase the depth of your page, or make a number of other compromises or revisions on your original rough. It is here, in this second stage that you develop a trained eye for the planning of type areas; so much so, that in time you will be surprised to learn how uncannily accurate you can be. You will also learn to stop fooling yourself, to stop allotting type to areas that just aren't there.

Then with the more accurate guide obtained from your first

cast, make a second layout and then a third and fourth until areas, space and color all begin to look and feel as you would like them to. Do not compromise on effort. Use tracing paper unsparingly. Work freely in the flowing stages of layout; work tightly in the exacting stages of fitting. Never work from memory of a typeface. Always have in mind the style or character of the type you would like to use and then take a look at the face itself in your specimen book. Have a showing of the type before you as you render the type form. Your type specimen books should always be within arm's reach.

2. Learn to look at a specimen showing of an alphabet with a very critical eye. Try to see the rhythm of the letter to see if there is any spottiness. Check such letters as "g, f, j, k, p, s, c, w, y" first in the roman and then in the italic, to see if they have idiosyncrasies that disturb you. Develop a "type" eye.

3. Type layout has to be worked at. At times it means the accurate tracing of letters to get the proper "feel" and "set" of the characters. This is always imperative when working with labels, logos, letterheads, title pages, and headlines. Learn to "set type" on a tracing pad, it is much cheaper and you can make all the changes you want at no expense but your own time.

It is a known fact that increasing the size of the typeface does not necessarily improve readability. It is fundamentally the space between lines that makes for easier reading. When the problem arises, do not be afraid of using smaller types such as 8, 9 and 10 point. The secret here is to use generous amounts of leading and white space. In trying to make the type more readable, too many designers usually make the type larger rather than increase the space between lines. Pages 108 and 109 are graphic examples of this point.

Here is a good guide: "the wider the measure, the larger the size of type" and "the narrower the measure, the smaller the size of type."

---

*The mathematical computation and fitting of manuscript copy into type areas.

In all instances where one-third of the size of body type can be specified for leading, a pleasing result is virtually guaranteed. This was Giambattista Bodoni's own rule and I have never found it wanting.

Type Specification

1. First have a layout. Neither good type specifications nor good layouts ever just happen. They are deliberately and carefully planned.

2. Select a typeface, taking into consideration:
  a. The nature of the message.
  b. The kind of art work that will accompany it.
  c. The process and paper on which it will be reproduced.
  d. Other typefaces that will appear in the same layout.
  e. The media to be used.
  f. Whether the type will stand alone or compete with other messages in surrounding environments.

Finally, in choosing a face for a given job the type director or artist must consider type color, legibility, and general style as well as size.

Next, it is important to check to see if the typeface you wish to use is possessed by the typographic house to which the job is being sent. Just to specify "Scotch Roman" is not enough. We must specify which Scotch Roman. This face is made by American Type Founders, Intertype Corporation, Mergenthaler Linotype Co., and Lanston Monotype Machine Co., and each foundry varies the face slightly.

Copy Fitting

Copy fitting is the mathematical translation of copy into type characters to fit the area provided for it in the layout. In order to cast the copy, the following data must first be determined:

  a. The number of characters in the copy.
  b. The character count (characters per pica) of the selected typeface.
  c. The area to be filled, width and depth.

By using available charts and aids, which provide the necessary information as to characters per pica in the given sizes and faces of type, we are able to determine how many lines our typewritten copy will make in the selected typeface and size. This is purely mathematical and not at all visual or difficult. All it takes is an ability to count and add correctly. Next, it is imperative that you convey to the typographer in plain simple language exactly what it is that you want. Mark your copy clearly and specify every detail in writing. Never let the typographer guess whether you want roman or italic, caps or lower case, indented or flushed lines. Specify the width of lines, amount of indentions and leading.

Bear in mind always that typography is based and charged for on a time basis. If your copy is so poorly marked that it takes the typographer an extra half hour to do your job, then that extra cost is the direct result of your inept marking and instructions.

A final point is to learn to use your faces economically. In linotype, for instance, learn what faces are combined on the same matrix. This information will enable you to use a range of machine typefaces with great economy. Avoid combining faces that do not align naturally. Aligning them is a costly practice, and can create problems on the printing press as well.

When you find that the suggestions listed above become a matter of habit, you can be sure that you are becoming professional.

WANT A GOOD DEAL?
OTHER DEALERS DON'T CARE?

CAREY
CARES

FIND OUT HOW MUCH AT
W. P. CAREY & CO.
28 BLOOMFIELD AVENUE
BLOOMFIELD, N. J., PI 3-3000
RENAULT & PEUGEOT

WANT A GOOD DEAL?
OTHER DEALERS DON'T CARE?

CAREY
CARES

FIND OUT HOW MUCH AT
W. P. CAREY & CO.
28 BLOOMFIELD AVENUE
BLOOMFIELD, N. J., PI 3-3000
RENAULT & PEUGEOT

SPACING

Avoid letter-spacing and wide word-spacing wherever possible. Do not letter-space lower case or script, unless intentional for open effects. Capital letters should be set optically tight and letter-spaced only when required. Wide word-spacing slows reading and destroys even tone and color. Do not penalize the typography because of one or two bad letter-combinations. Alphabets were designed with letters intended to fit together harmoniously. Letter-spacing introduces "letters of white space" and destroys the original color of the font.

Many typographers will disagree with this theory. In their opinion, proper space between the poorest combination of letters is the determining factor for the spacing to be followed throughout an entire job. However, when working with reproduction proofs use a razor blade to "cut in" and adjust bad letter combinations.

Optical spacing is always a personal thing; no two people will ever agree on this point. If there is close agreement let it go and move on.

It is not necessary that there be total agreement on this subject. Spacing must **feel** right. This is something that comes only through experience and working with type.

It is good training to trace the same lines on tracing paper, increasing or decreasing the space between lines, letters, and words until you begin to arrive consistently at a satisfactory style of spacing that is reflective of your own particular taste. Squint your eyes when spacing. This will help you to see the over-all color and will show the uneven or spotty color of bad spacing or alignment.

The examples on these two pages show marked improvement wherever excessive word space has been removed and corrected.

HAVE A FREE TRIP
TO EUROPE ON
THE FRENCH LINE

(BEFORE)

HAVE A FREE TRIP
TO EUROPE ON
THE FRENCH LINE

(AFTER)

West Side:
Broadway and 62 Street, JU 2-6885
East Side:
425 Park Ave. (56 Street) PL 1-3550
Woodside, Queens:
70-65 Queens Boulevard, DE 5-0520

(BEFORE)

West Side:
Broadway and 62 Street, JU 2-6885
East Side:
425 Park Ave. (56 Street) PL 1-3550
Woodside, Queens:
70-65 Queens Boulevard, DE 5-0520

(AFTER)

(MECHANICAL)

THE
DUNGEON
OF
THE
HEART

(OPTICAL)

THE
DUNGEON
OF
THE
HEART

ALIGNMENT

Mechanical alignment versus optical alignment: We must try to remember that everything we see on a type page has been assembled by a typesetter. Ordinary typesetting is the "mechanical" setting of type . . ."optical" setting of type is the art of typography.

In vertical alignments check for the alignment at the left and the right edges. Check to see that such capital letters as A, C, G, J, O, Q, S, T, V, W, X, Y, have been adjusted optically to compensate for their irregular forms.

In the examples shown above, right, the first and fourth lines have been moved optically to the left to permit the top strokes of the "T's" to extend further into the margin, thereby permitting the eye to form a perfect, optical, flush-left alignment.

(BEFORE)

PRICES: DAUPHINE $1645, 4 CV $1345.
PEUGEOT "403" SEDAN $2250, AND THE
PEUGEOT "403" STATION WAGON $2490
LO. MI.   ALL PRICES P. O. E.

(AFTER)

PRICES: DAUPHINE $1645, 4 CV $1345.
PEUGEOT "403" SEDAN $2250, AND THE
PEUGEOT "403" STATION WAGON $2490
LO. MI.   ALL PRICES P.O. E.

PUNCTUATION

In vertical alignments, wherever possible "hang" such punctuation marks as periods, commas, open quotes and apostrophes in the margins. Do not "hang" exclamation marks or question marks and only rarely should colons, semicolons or parentheses be "hung." The purpose of "hanging" the punctuation is to create optical alignments. Get out of the habit of mechanical typography, typography must look right—optically.

When lines are to be centered vertically, always center type optically with those lines above and below in mind and adjust for punctuation marks as described above.

There are always exceptions to the rule. For instance, when there are more than ten or fifteen lines of text, the fine point of "hung" punctuation can be ignored. The eye no longer will be disturbed by the lack of such refinements, for it will see only the mass of lines.

In the examples shown above, the periods at the ends of lines have not been "hung" in the "before" example. The lines therefore appear to be indented on the right edge. Notice the improvement in the corrected version.

A frequent accident that occurs in typography is the use of the figure zero "0," in place of the capital letter "O" or vice versa. Notice that in the fourth line of the top setting the figure has been used in place of the cap "O" in the word "LO." Very often designers will purposely use the "O" in place of the figure zero, or the cap "I" in place of the figure "1." This is particularly true in a sans serif setting.

(BEFORE)

AD JUST
UNNING
LE ROSE,
Y, BASIN
ME AND
NG, LOV-
ED OVER
Y-DRESS-
SEE. I'M
WALLER,
TH ONE
AT THE
TA ASK,
UM SAT
NG BEER
AID THE
R. "WITH-
S BLIND
ILDREN
PIANO."

(AFTER)

AD JUST
UNNING
LE ROSE,
Y, BASIN
ME AND
NG, LOV-
ED OVER
Y-DRESS-
SEE. I'M
WALLER,
TH ONE
AT THE
TA ASK,
UM SAT
NG BEER
AID THE
R. "WITH-
S BLIND
ILDREN
PIANO."

(BEFORE)

Reach, pardner, for the big news:

(AFTER)

Reach, pardner, for the big news:

(AFTER) Revised

Reach, pardner, for the big news:

PUNCTUATION (continued)

''Perfect'' typography must be unorthodox typography. It may mean using wrong fonts, cutting hyphens in half, using smaller punctuation marks, in fact, doing anything that is needed to improve the appearance of typography.

On page 96 the punctuation marks have been set smaller in the ''after'' setting. This seems to improve the appearance of the right edge. However, while the column on the right may appear better when shown in this manner as a fragment, the reader is advised to refer back to pages 44 and 45, on which the entire column of typography is shown. One then has to question whether or not the punctuation on the left is more suitable when viewed in that mass.

Nevertheless, the ''after'' examples would seem to justify the use of smaller punctuation marks when used in such narrow columns. In the bottom example shown on this page, the commas and colon have been set in an extra condensed sans serif face. Although the commas on the first line appear to be acceptable, it is questionable whether the colon is entirely satisfactory. Notice how much extra space appears between the two dots of the colon. In this case it might be more desirable to retain the colon used in the ''before'' setting. Therefore a combination of the two refinements would be in order.

(BEFORE)

Joan Le-wan-dow-ska representing
Carl Fischer, photographer; Edward
Sorel, illustrator; 421 east 54 street New
York City, N.Y., telephone MU 8-2828

(AFTER)

Joan Le-wan-dow-ska representing
Carl Fischer, photographer; Edward
Sorel, illustrator; 421 east 54 street New
York City, N.Y., telephone MU 8-2828

PUNCTUATION (continued)

Figures of punctuation have often been designed that do not seem to be consistent and in harmony with other letters of the same font. It is up to the designer, therefore, to compensate for these irregularities by using figures of punctuation from other fonts. In this "before" example, the commas used were much bolder than the period within the same font. The typeface used is Calson 540. Notice that this incongruity also appears in the semicolon.

In the corrected example, compensation has been made by using commas and semicolons from a Baskerville font. The weight and color of these punctuation marks blend perfectly with the rest of the type and therefore are acceptable. (Of course the point can always be argued that the bolder commas add a distinctive note to the font. Since this can both be questioned and argued without any real benefit, it becomes purely a matter of choice.

(BEFORE)

this
magazine
today

this
magazine
today

this
magazine
today

(AFTER)

this
magazine
today

this
magazine
today

this
magazine
today

UNDERSCORES

The underscore is a point of emphasis. It belongs to whatever word it underlines. Therefore the underscore should be set as close as possible to the word it emphasizes. The examples shown above are good guides for underscore setting. Not only are the underscores cut in as close to the type as possible but they are of a weight that does not detract from the typeface itself. (Since this cannot always be accomplished, particularly with hand type, it is often advisable to rule the underscore in by hand.) Very often underscores similar to the weight of the typeface used do not provide additional contrast and only serve to clog the space between lines. Wherever possible a light underscore should be used with all light faces, and for bold faces one that is approximately one-half the thickness of the weight of the face (and possibly lighter still).

THE OLD WAY:	Ya Ye Yo Y. Wa We Wo W. Va Ve Vo V. Ta Te To Tw Tu Ty ffa ffe ffo
THE LOGOTYPE WAY:	Ya Ye Yo Y. Wa We Wo W. Va Ve Vo V. Ta Te To Tw Tu Ty ffa ffe ffo
THE OLD WAY:	Yard, Yellow, Yours, Wander, Welcome, New York, Woman, W. Vance, Vellum, Volume.
THE LOGOTYPE WAY:	Yard, Yellow, Yours, Wander, Welcome, New York, Woman, W. Vance, Vellum, Volume.

TYPOGRAPHIC REFINEMENTS

Letter combinations such as Yo, Wa, and Ve, have always been an eyesore to good composition. In setting type by hand, it is extremely difficult to cut and fit such cap and lower case letters together to eliminate the unsightly gaps. The expense of doing this work when attempted in body composition is excessive. However, the various manufacturers of matrices for typesetting machines have developed a series of logotypes and ligatures which make it possible to eliminate this eyesore.

The logotype is not merely a refinement for connoisseurs of typography. The layman, who may not know just what it is in a page of typography that makes it agreeable to him, will sense the improvement resulting from the closing up of these gaps.

Shown here are letter combinations cut in both the old and new logotype way. Also shown are some word specimens set both with and without logotypes.

In the construction industry, conventional concepts of materials are now being enlarged by research in chemistry and physics. Scientific discoveries are giving to the architect a new freedom in designing for beauty and function. Significant research in the molecular remodeling of matter is already well under way. New building materials are being formed having the lightness, the structural integrity and the economy inherent in natural phenomena such as an egg shell, a crystal, a leaf. Again, in the basic field of industrial gases, technical advances in such areas as medicine, electronics, space flight research, high energy fuels, metallurgy, nuclear science and cryogenics (extremely low-temperature research) have extended tonnage requirements and have widened uses. New market requirements have stimulated research and development leading to more efficient production and distribution of industrial and medical gases. Few supplier industries have been so directly affected by such a wide variety of scientific activities in areas of great technological innovation as the compressed gas industry. Many new developments in food processing, medicine, and in a wide variety of industrial production techniques have been made possible by increased knowledge and expanded capabilities in gas dynamics. As a result, sales of industrial and medical gases have increased substantially during every year of the past decade. In one field alone—the very active scientific area of cryogenics—there are in progress developments which depend upon certain of the basic industrial

TEXT SETTING

(JUSTIFIED MEASURES) Whenever a body of text is set flush at both the left and right edges, it is virtually impossible to have even word spacing in all lines. (Newspaper typesetting is an excellent example of very poor word spacing.) However, take pains to see that the spacing between words is as close and even as possible. In setting columns that are flush left and flush right, hyphenate at the end of a line wherever possible, rather than increase the space between words to avoid hyphenations.

Hyphens were made for such purposes—use them! The penalty for such hyphenations is more than offset by the reward in over-all

color and texture. Wide word spacing slows reading, creates rivers in paragraphs, makes for bad color, and results in poor typography.

Refinement practices such as "hanging" punctuation marks in the margin and using smaller marks of punctuation is not necessary in a deep setting of text. In addition to being too costly, whenever a text setting exceeds 10 or 12 lines in depth the eye no longer appreciates such refinements. The eye grasps the entire column as a unit and does not focus on individual lines.

A

In the construction industry,
conventional concepts of materials
are now being enlarged by
research in chemistry and physics.
Scientific discoveries are giving
to the architect a new freedom in
designing for beauty and
function. Significant research in
the molecular remodeling of
matter is already well under way.
New building materials are
being formed having the lightness,
the structural integrity and
the economy inherent in natural
phenomena such as an egg shell,
a crystal, a leaf. Again, in the basic
field of industrial gases, technical
advances in such areas as medicine,
electronics, space flight research,
high energy fuels, metallurgy,
nuclear science and cryogenics
(extremely low-temperature
research) have extended tonnage
requirements and have widened
uses. New market requirements
have stimulated research and
development leading to more
efficient production and
distribution of industrial and
medical gases. Few supplier
industries have been so directly
affected by such a wide variety of
scientific activities in areas of
great technological innovation as
the compressed gas industry.
Many new developments in food
processing, medicine, and in a
wide variety of industrial production
techniques have been made
possible by increased knowledge
and expanded capabilities in
gas dynamics. As a result, sales of
industrial and medical gases have
increased substantially during every
year of the past decade. In one
field alone—the very active scientific
area of cryogenics—there are in
progress developments which depend
upon certain of the basic industrial

B

In the construction industry, conventional concepts of materials are now
being enlarged by research in chemistry
and physics. Scientific discoveries are
giving to the architect a new freedom
in designing for beauty and function.
Significant research in the molecular
remodeling of matter is already well
under way. New building materials are
being formed having the lightness, the
structural integrity and the economy
inherent in natural phenomena such as
an egg shell, a crystal, a leaf. Again,
in the basic field of industrial gases,
technical advances in such areas as
medicine, electronics, space flight research, high energy fuels, metallurgy,
nuclear science and cryogenics (extremely low-temperature research) have
extended tonnage requirements and
have widened uses. New market requirements have stimulated research and
development leading to more efficient
production and distribution of industrial and medical gases. Few supplier
industries have been so directly affected
by such a wide variety of scientific
activities in areas of great technological
innovation as the compressed gas industry. Many new developments in food
processing, medicine, and in a wide
variety of industrial production techniques have been made possible by
increased knowledge and expanded
capabilities in gas dynamics. As a result, sales of industrial and medical
gases have increased substantially
during every year of the past decade.
In one field alone—the very active
scientific area of cryogenics—there are
in progress developments which depend
upon certain of the basic industrial

C

how pretty I. Miller stockings are. Blended exclusively for I. Miller shoe colors, perfect for new clothes—and your legs, which after all are your most important fashion accessories. Seamed, seamless, sheerness after sheerness, ordinary prices—fantastic flattery! In frosted white boxes of three.

D

how pretty I. Miller stockings are. Blended exclusively for I. Miller shoe colors, perfect for new clothes—and your legs, which after all are your most important fashion accessories. Seamed, seamless, sheerness after sheerness, ordinary prices—fantastic flatter- In frosted white boxes of three.

E

how pretty I. Miller stockings are. Blended exclusively for I. Miller shoe colors, perfect for new clothes—and your legs, which after all are your most important fashion accessories Seamed, seamless, sheerness after sheerness, ordinary prices—fantastic flattery! In frosted white boxes of three.

RAGGED LINES

In setting copy flush left and ragged right, or vice versa, word spacing should be consistent. There should be only a slight variation in the length of lines. A ragged setting should look as if it were a piece of paper torn loosely from top to bottom. Once again the rule: **Set tight.** Unjustified setting offers the greatest opportunity for perfect typography; for with no flush-left, flush-right justification necessary to adhere to, all word spacing can be identical and should be no more than the width of a lower case "r."

The examples shown on page 102 are set in the same face and have the same leading. In both cases the copy is identical to that used on page 101.

In examples A and B the word spacing is uniform and good. However, the excessively ragged edge in example A is very poor; it destroys the tone and color within the column. Example B has been set properly; the result is a column of text that is "softer" to look at and inviting to read.

The examples on page 103 show the restrictions of a narrow measure for both justified and ragged settings. Example C is very poorly set. Example D is slightly better but example E is the best. Increasing the width of the measure improved the over-all color and made for easier reading.

In ragged setting it is always best to avoid hyphenations wherever possible. However, the question always arises as to which is more important, that a text **be** easy to read, or **look** easy to read.

E VERY WEEK the New York Philhar- monic does play in almost every town across America, over CBS Radio. No one has to stir from home. No one has to buy a ticket. A radio is your front seat.

D O YOU REALIZE how many CBS Radio programs are worthy of being made assignments for spe- cific classroom discussion? Make it a habit to glance at your local daily radio schedules. For just to point out

E VERY WEEK the New York Philhar- monic does play in almost every town across America, over CBS Radio. No one has to stir from home. No one has to buy a ticket. A radio is your front seat.

D O YOU REALIZE how many CBS Radio programs are worthy of being made assignments for spe- cific classroom discussion? Make it a habit to glance at your local daily radio schedules. For just to point out

INITIALS

The use of large initials in text matter requires very careful handling. The attempt to create perfect alignments is always fraught with such problems as line leading and irregular letter forms in the initials. Here, the top two examples have been set improperly. The bottom two show the corrected version.

The top setting creates an optical box within which the initial is framed. The eye therefore grasps the initial and then wanders in an effort to pick up the first word. The corrected version places the first line of text as close to the initial as possible so that the eye moves more easily into the paragraph. The use of small caps creates an optical horizontal alignment which is very pleasing when aligned with the top of the large initial. (These examples were taken from page 68 of this book and the reader should refer to the comments for that page.)

9 pt. Bodoni Bold Small Caps, Lino.
with 9 pt. Century Schoolbook, 5 pt. leaded

THE PRINTER'S POWER. Greece had her temples and Europe her grand Renaissance age. Each was the art expression of its time and place. Both gave art and beauty to the people; brought it into their everyday life; got them to thinking about it and eventually wanting it and living it. But today business through the printing craft is largely the channel which brings BEAUTY and ART into our daily lives; introduces it into every home; puts it upon our

THE PRINTER'S POWER. Greece had her temples and Europe her grand Renaissance age. Each was the art expression of its time and place. Both gave art and beauty to the people; both brought it into their everyday life; got them to thinking about it and eventually wanting it and living it. But today business through the printing craft is largely the channel which brings BEAUTY and ART into our daily lives; introduces it into every home; puts it upon our

8 pt. Standard Bold Caps
with 9 pt. Century Schoolbook, 5 pt. leaded

SELECTING AND COMBINING TYPEFACES

The measurement of type color; color balance between text and display, and between type and illustration; leading; letter spacing; and word spacing are all areas for consideration in selecting typefaces.

But aside from aesthetic reasons, paper, color, and printing process will frequently determine the selection of type, therefore, the designer must approach each problem separately.

The selection of a body text is no problem. Any face can be used successfully so long as the width of the line is pleasing and the leading between lines is comfortable. A problem always arises when there are more than two faces to be used within the same text setting. So many factors enter into the decision that the designer cannot always use a previously successful combination as the solution for another problem.

The selection of bold lead-in heads to be used with running text is probably the most common problem for the designer.

The basic considerations that govern the selection of a second bold face are that there be alignment with the body text, that the weight not overpower the text, and if color is to be used in the type, that the decision be made accordingly.

On pages 105, 106 and 107, one body text has been used consistently throughout, 9 pt Century Schoolbook, 5 pt leaded. The examples shown all contain suggested heads for this body text. Not all the suggestions shown are economical due to the fact that some are set by hand and require cutting-in of the linotype slugs. However, these examples indicate clearly some of the many possibilities the designer has at his disposal.

Art has its own position in industry and it need not necessarily be what is known as commercial art; it need only be art. When business men thoroughly learn that art can be itself and still be useful to them; when they cease distorting it in the effort to adapt it to business; **then only will they realize its full commercial value.** Let the artist remain an artist and the business man a business man; but let them understand each other thoroughly and always work together for better understanding

9 pt. News Gothic Bold Lino with 9 pt. Century Schoolbook

Art has its own position in industry and it need not necessarily be what is known as commercial art; it need only be art. When business men thoroughly learn that art can be itself and still be useful to them; when they cease distorting it in the effort to adapt it to business; **then only will they realize its full commercial value.** Let the artist remain an artist and the business man a business man; but let them understand each other thoroughly and always work together for better understanding

9 pt. Akzidenz Grotesk Medium Lino with 9 Pt. Century Schoolbook

Art has its own position in industry and it need not necessarily be what is known as commercial art; it need only be art. When business men thoroughly learn that art can be itself and still be useful to them; when they cease distorting it in the effort to adapt it to business; **then only will they realize its full commercial value.** Let the artist remain an artist and the business man a business man; but let them understand each other thoroughly and always work together for better under-

8 pt. Franklin Gothic Lino with 9 pt. Century Schoolbook

9 pt. Bodoni Bold Lino with 9 pt. Century Schoolbook

Art has its own position in industry and it need not necessarily be what is known as commercial art; it need only be art. When business men thoroughly learn that art can be itself and still be useful to them; when they cease distorting it in the effort to adapt it to business; **then only will they realize its full commercial value.** Let the artist remain an artist and the business man a business man; but let them understand each other thoroughly and always work together for better under-

10 pt. Melior Semi-Bold with 9 pt. Century Schoolbook

Art has its own position in industry and it need not necessarily be what is known as commercial art; it need only be art. When business men thoroughly learn that art can be itself and still be useful to them; when they cease distorting it in the effort to adapt it to business; **then only will they realize its full commercial value.** Let the artist remain an artist and the business man a business man; but let them understand each other thoroughly and always work together for better under-

10 pt. Times Roman Bold Mono with 9 pt. Century Schoolbook

Art has its own position in industry and it need not necessarily be what is known as commercial art; it need only be art. When business men thoroughly learn that art can be itself and still be useful to them; when they cease distorting it in the effort to adapt it to business; **then only will they realize its full commercial value.** Let the artist remain an artist and the business man a business man; but let them understand each other thoroughly and always work together for better under-

There are many definitions of beauty by poets and philosophers. We are conscious of beauty when there is a harmonious relation between something in our nature and the quality of the object which delights us. Beauty is not the starting point, but the point of arrival; a thing can only be beautiful if it is true. Truth itself is only a complete harmony, and harmony is finally only a bundle of utilities. There is a beauty in mechanical fitness which no art can enhance. The world has been made beautiful by be-

4 PT LEADED

There are many definitions of beauty by poets and philosophers. We are conscious of beauty when there is a harmonious relation between something in our nature and the quality of the object which delights us. Beauty is not the starting point, but the point of arrival; a thing can only be beautiful if it is true. Truth itself is only a complete harmony, and harmony is finally only a bundle of utilities. There is a beauty in mechanical fitness which no art can enhance. The world has been made beautiful by being gradually divested of every ornament

5 PT LEADED

There are many definitions of beauty by poets and philosophers. We are conscious of beauty when there is a harmonious relation between something in our nature and the quality of the object which delights us. Beauty is not the starting point, but the point of arrival; a thing can only be beautiful if it is true. Truth itself is only a complete harmony, and harmony is finally only a bundle of utilities. There is a beauty in mechanical fitness which no art can enhance. The world has been made beautiful by being gradually divested of every ornament which was not fitted to endure. There may be

6 PT LEADED

There are many definitions of beauty by poets and philosophers. We are conscious of beauty when there is a harmonious relation between something in our nature and the quality of the object which delights us. Beauty is not the starting point, but the point of arrival; a thing can only be beautiful if it is true. Truth itself is only a complete harmony, and harmony is finally a bundle of utilities. There is a beauty in mechanical fitness which no art can enhance. The world has been

3 PT LEADED

There are many definitions of beauty by poets and philosophers. We are conscious of beauty when there is a harmonious relation between something in our nature and the quality of the object which delights us. Beauty is not the starting point, but the point of arrival; a thing can only be beautiful if it is true. Truth itself is only a complete harmony, and harmony is finally only a bundle of utilities. There

2 PT LEADED

LEADING

Shown on this spread are five columns of text all set to the same measure but in different point sizes of two families of type, News Gothic (regular) and News Gothic Condensed. The important thing to remember is that instead of increasing the size of type for greater readability, one ought to think first of increasing the leading between lines. Observe for yourself those columns that appear easiest to read. The inclination might be to choose the smallest of the settings. In the smaller settings the eye seems to focus inward and to encompass a group of lines at one time, while in the larger settings the eye seems to be drawn outward and it is difficult to grasp more than a few words at a time.

The purpose of these examples is not to make large type look more difficult to read, but to prove the point that small type with proper leading is not necessarily difficult to read.

dedication

To typographers, designers and students. To all those whose
love of beautiful typography sustains and encourages
skilled contemporary craftsmanship. And especially to those
typographers who care enough to uphold the traditions
of their craft, who constantly pursue perfection. Only through a
blend of fine design and sensitive interpretation can today's
artists and craftsmen perform their most significant function—
improvement in the aesthetics and mechanics of typography.

acknowledgments

With grateful appreciation to Sol M. Cantor, Harry Gloates,
Herman Kass, and the late Alexander Ross; without their
guidance and generously shared knowledge, this book
could not have been written.
To Frank Canner and Russell Etter, my thanks for their significant
personal assistance.
And deep appreciation to my many colleagues and associates,
whose active interest and creative ideas have contributed so much
to the inspiration of this book.

_____

Specimens shown on pages 5, 11, 25, 31, 32, 44, 48, 49, and 62
are from a series of exercises in experimental typography for which
special "librettos" were written by Percy Seitlin. Excerpts from
the text reprinted through the courtesy of the author.

about the author

Aaron Burns, President and Director of Design of Graphic Arts
Typographers, Inc., New York, is one of the leading consultants in
typographic design in America. With a broad background in
the field of visual and graphic communication as a designer, art
director and educator, he is especially qualified to write on the
subject of typography.

Born in Passaic, N. J. he studied at the Newark School of Fine and
Industrial Art and Brigham Young University. After the war he worked
as a designer and art director for the late Alexander Ross,
Sudler and Hennessey, Inc., and Monogram Art Studio in New York.
He has been a free lance consultant in design and typography
since 1949, associated first with Empire State Craftsmen, Inc., and
from 1954 to 1961 with The Composing Room, Inc. of New York.

His interest in education has been actively expressed in his work
with the Type Directors Club of New York, and as an instructor
in Advanced and Experimental Typographic Design at Pratt Institute
since 1955. As a member and Educational Chairman of the Type
Directors Club in 1955 he organized the series of lectures,
"Inspired Typography '26-'66"; was Chairman of the first world
seminar on typographic design, "The Art and Science of Typography"
at Silvermine, Conn., in 1958; and in 1959 was chairman of the
forum "Typography U.S.A." in New York City.

A recipient of numerous design awards, he has been a frequent
lecturer before art directors clubs, schools and professional
organizations throughout the country.

He is now the Director of the newly founded International Center for
the Typographic Arts, New York. He is also a member of l'Association
Typographique Internationale, Paris-Geneva; Compagnon de Lure,
France; Type Directors Club of New York, American Institute
of Graphic Arts; and Art Directors Club of New York.

—JEAN KOEFOED, REINHOLD PUBLISHING CORP., INC.

designers

typeface page index

table of contents

Text set in News Gothic with News Gothic Bold and printed by offset lithography on 80 lb. Warren's Offset Enamel Dull.

Specimen pages set by The Composing Room, Inc., New York; Graphic Arts Typographers, Inc., New York; and N.V. Drukkerij G.J.J. Thieme, The Netherlands